LAOTSE, WALDO, AND ME

ALSO BY MARGARET EMERSON

Breathing Underwater:
The Inner Life of T'ai Chi Ch'uan
North Atlantic Books, Berkeley CA

A Potter's Notes on Tai Chi Chuan
Artichoke Press, Bayside CA

"Wu T'ai Chi, Kao Style:
As Practiced and Taught by Margaret Emerson"
(DVD)
Artichoke Press, Bayside CA

Eyes of the Mirror
(a memoir)
Artichoke Press, Bayside CA

MARGARET EMERSON WEBSITE
www.MARGARETEMERSON.com

CONTACT THE AUTHOR BY E-MAIL
margaretemerson@att.net

LAOTSE, WALDO, AND ME

Margaret Emerson

Artichoke Press
Bayside, California

ISBN 978-0-9620690-1-7

Excerpts as submitted: #39 [51.], 41 [101.], 53 [121.], 64 [51.] from TAO TE CHING BY LAO TZU, A NEW ENGLISH VERSION, WITH FOREWORD AND NOTES, by STEPHEN MITCHELL. Translation copyright © 1988 by Stephen Mitchell. Reprinted by permission of HarperCollins Publishers.

Excerpt as submitted: Chapter 65, (p. 174) from TAO: A NEW WAY OF THINKING, translation copyright © 1975 by Chang Chung-yuan. Reprinted by permission of HarperCollins Publishers.

"Verse 76," "Verse 36," "Verse 50," and "Verse 52" from TAO TE CHING: THE DEFINITIVE EDITION by Lao Tzu, translated by Jonathan Star, translation copyright © 2001 by Jonathan Star. Used by permission of Tarcher, an imprint of Penguin Publishing Group, a division of Penguin Random House LLC. All rights reserved.

"Verse Two," "Verse Twenty," "Verse Twenty-Five," and "Verse Fifty-Two" from TAO TE CHING by Lao Tsu, translated by Gia-fu Feng and Jane English, copyright renewed 2000 by Carol Wilson and Jane English. Used by permission of Alfred A. Knopf, an imprint of the Knopf Doubleday Publishing Group, a division of Penguin Random House LLC. All rights reserved.

Excerpts from Chapter 3, (p. 56), Chapter 67, (pp. 291-2), Chapter 54, (p. 249) from THE WISDOM OF LAOTSE by Laotse, translated by Lin Yutang, copyright © 1948 by Random House, Inc., copyright renewed 1976 by Lin Yutang. Used by permission of Hsiang Ju Lin.

Cover painting by Margaret Emerson

Published by
Artichoke Press
P.O. Box 16
Bayside, California 95524

Visit www.margaretemerson.com.

Printed in the United States of America

CONTENTS

PREFACE

*Where can I find a man who has forgotten words so
I can have a word with him?
--Chuangtse, Taoist philosopher fourth century BCE*

How perfect that my table is round. Like place settings at
a dinner party, I arranged each of my eight translations of the
Tao Te Ching. They'd come into my life gradually, casually, and
mostly randomly as I browsed used book stores during thirty-six
years of practicing T'ai Chi. It occurred to me that it would be
fun to read them all at once, moving my chair from one to the
other, making a full circuit with each chapter. The vivid hologram
of Laotse that emerged was riveting; it felt like I was having a
prolonged dinner conversation with him—the kind where you
lose track of time. I'd been reading Ralph Waldo Emerson in-
termittently all my life and was struck by the parallels between
them, so I invited Emerson to the party. The fact is I was starved
for conversation on ideas and observations that have filled my
head, heart, and gut over a lifetime. I wanted to talk to Laotse
and Emerson about them.

What do age and time matter? Laotse was 2,500 years old; Waldo (the name he preferred) was over 200; I was 65. We were all intensely eager to talk and we were all good listeners. The conversation rolled like a leisurely train pausing at one station after another, connected by meandering rails.

Laotse's *Tao Te Ching*—a mere 5,000 words—was the hub and catalyst of the discussion. Using poetry and paradox, he turns our gaze toward the ineffable Tao in which the material and immaterial worlds are all one thing. Within this unity is the tug and pull of opposites—yin and yang—and a constant search for balance while riding the inevitable, ceaseless cycle of growth and decay. Taoism is about going with the circular flow (not against it) and harmonizing ourselves with nature, starting with our own nature.

We know only the bare bones of Laotse's life. Born in 571 BCE, he was a contemporary of Confucius (who had a very different worldview). Laotse was a librarian—the Keeper of the Royal Archives for the court of Zhou—so he had access to the Taoist classics of the time. He married and had children. During his career, he earned the name Laotse meaning "old venerable," and had followers, but no interest in founding a school. At midlife or perhaps later, weary of civilization and foreseeing yet another war, he retired and disappeared into the mountains. The legend is that when he arrived at the western gate of the kingdom dis-guised as a farmer, the sentry recognized him and asked him to write down his collected wisdom before leaving. Laotse complied and thus we have the eighty-one concise, gemlike chapters of the *Tao Te Ching*.

Compared to the bare bones of Laotse's history, we have the detailed anatomy of Emerson's. He provided us with thousands of pages of essays, poems, journals, and letters. Emerson is more earthy (Laotse sets a low bar for earthiness) and more concrete, but can be just as poetic and intuitive. In addition to his own words, volumes have been written about the man, from contemporaries up to the present day.

Emerson is often remembered as a Unitarian, but he resigned from the church when he was twenty-nine, after about six years of preaching. It was around this time that one of his brothers asked him, "So what religion are you, anyway?" He answered—after a long uncharacteristic pause—that he was closest to the Quakers. A few years later he was a founding member of the Transcendental Club. It didn't take him long to transcend the fanaticism of his fellow Transcendentalists. Emerson was profoundly influenced by the work of Persian and Hindu mystics. And although the *Tao Te Ching* was not translated into English during Emerson's lifetime, his mature essays, "Circles" and "The Over-Soul" are fundamentally Taoist. Ultimately he was an experimentalist.

All three of us are careless of labels. We sense that underneath one mystery is another mystery—and another and another. Our joy is in roaming about aimlessly in this vast space, bumping into particles (clues) here and there and being ignited by them. Happily there is no end to it.

Both Laotse and Emerson talk about unlearning—throwing away the books and simply looking outward to the natural world and inward to the natural world in order to be guided and supported. I've been constantly aware of the irony that this writing has required massive reading on my part. I'm seeking wisdom and advice on how to live by reading and rereading the words of people who tell me to stop reading. Well, they read a lot too while coming around to that conclusion. I love these two men; I'm drawn to them; I have to read them so we can have our dinner conversation. Laotse, Emerson, and I don't always agree, but that adds spice to the menu.

I'm in my late sixties and although I've always been a contemplative person, this is a time for me to be turning further inward—doing more T'ai Chi, meditation, and qigong; and putting myself where I can absorb unspoiled nature. It's a time to stop striving. That's why I decided this book would either write itself or not get written at all. I would not push; I would not force it. Indeed, it's fun like a thousand-piece jigsaw puzzle is fun. Laotse would like this approach—it's very wu-wei: effortless effort.

Reading multiple versions of the *Tao Te Ching* has taught me that no one knows for sure what Laotse meant to say. Not only did he write in an ancient language that no modern Chinese scholar can pretend to decode with absolute certainty, he also wrote in poetry—impressionistic and minimalistic. A scholar contemporary with Laotse would have had to draw on intuition in order to grasp his meaning. And intuition comes out of an individual's unique core. So each translation is shaped by the intellect and intuition of the translator (and they argue with each other in their introductions and notes). I enjoy watching this play out—not only in my reading, but also in my own interpretation of Laotse. I freely choose particular parts of particular chapters by particular translators to gerrymander my own Taoist philosophy according to Laotse. It can be hard to know the difference between what we think Laotse means and what we'd like him to mean.

Adding to the cross currents in my brain is the awareness that neither of these men (particularly Emerson) always agreed with himself. They didn't allow a foolish consistency to hobble their thinking. While reading a sermon, Emerson paused, looked up at his congregation, said, "I no longer believe that last sentence," then went back to his text and sailed on.

I have to say that there's a malevolent cloud bearing down heavily on me as I work on this book. Way beyond knowing there are too many words out there already, and people have been saying the same things for millennia to little effect, this is something else. I've always thought of writing as potentially timeless, potentially for posterity. It's an assumption that comes out of reading (talking to) so many writers who are long dead.

But what if there's no posterity? The prospect is deflating and demoralizing. We humans are industriously destroying our planet—or at least destroying its ability to support human life.

I'm human; therefore I'm guilty. This is unbearable: To imagine my precious Crater Lake (the love of my life), losing its clarity, its otherworldly blue at the hands of humans and the metastasized cancer of global warming.

I used to think of us as a failed species, but then I decided we're just a species like any other—progressing along the usual cycle of growth and decay. We carry within ourselves the seeds of our own destruction; there are too many of us; we're too selfish and greedy. There are many problems we can identify and try to solve, but the root problem is the nature of human nature. Or is it? Humans haven't always lived this way. Can we bring ourselves back to Laotse's "Grand Harmony," the Neolithic cultures of cooperation instead of domination?

Whether or not I believe that's possible, I choose to behave as if I have hope—to exert my small influence when I can. A primal loyalty will not allow me to abandon myself, my friends, my community, my species, or my planet. Maybe my ninety-eight-year-old friend (a historian) is right that humans are surprisingly resilient and resourceful. Still, even he acknowledges that there will be growing, unnecessary chaos and suffering before we bring ourselves back into balance with ourselves and our environment.

I find solace in knowing that I'm not only human. My dreams, visions, meditation, and T'ai Chi keep showing me that I'm equally part of the indestructible, inexhaustible Tao. I am—we are—transcendent.

Margaret Emerson

A Note on Pronouns

All but one of the translations of the *Tao Te Ching* that I quote from use male pronouns throughout. Emerson also uses exclusively male pronouns. In the interest of balance and affirmative action, I use female pronouns when speaking in my own voice.

When, in my imagination, I substitute female pronouns in the material I'm quoting, the writer's words strike me directly and penetrate deeper, instead of hitting me obliquely and glancing off. I feel a much stronger connection to the author's meaning and a sense of relief that I am really the person being spoken to—the author sees me.

I choose to use female pronouns when not quoting others until I'm ready to viscerally accept a pronoun as truly genderless. At this point, using "they" and "their" (always plural) is not meeting that requirement. We need to invent and get used to a new, genderless pronoun that has both a singular and plural form.

ONE

THE TAO

I like the word "Way" to interpret "Tao" in English. Tao is the way things work, the way things move, and if you follow the Tao, it opens up a way. No destination, just a path. I can dive into it, give myself up to it, allow myself to ripple gently or gush with abandon. It leads; I follow. Have you ever watched a leaf bob along lazily for a while and then suddenly spin furiously on the currents of a creek or river? "We are as men in a balloon," Emerson says, "and do not think so much of the point we have left, or the point we would make, as of the liberty and glory of the way."[1]

The Tao, however, can't be captured by a word. Laotse begins by saying the Tao is unnameable, indescribable. If you try to name it, it has already escaped your grasp. It contains the material world yet it is not material. (How do we get our heads around that?) It is the "Mother of All Things." When we are in a rare state of emptiness and clarity, stripped of desire and intention, we can glimpse this mystery. As our ordinary, desirous, striving selves we see only the manifestations of the Tao—the material world.[2]

The Tao has no limits. Emerson quotes St. Augustine as saying the nature of God is a circle whose center is everywhere and its circumference nowhere.[3] Circumference and center are linked to each other. With no circumference, there is no fixed center. Through my practices, I receive that each one of us (and everything else in the universe) is *simultaneously* the center of the Tao. Everything is part of a ubiquitous web of boundless potential. What occurs in one point reverberates in all other points. And we—and all components of the web—have access to the dynamism of every thread and every point.

That's because the Tao is unity, identity; it is One. It is a pregnant void.

One gives birth to Two—yin and yang, complementary opposing forces. I watch these forces work with each gesture of T'ai Chi. It's simultaneous cause and effect. Every upward and outward block, strike, or kick is supported and made possible by an equal and opposite downward, inward sinking. We all know that if we want to get up from a chair, we don't just levitate. We have to push downward on the ground with our feet in order to rise up. The T'ai Chi classics say, "In up there is down." Physicists say for every action there is an equal and opposite reaction. Yin and yang could not exist without each other; they're two sides of the same coin.

And these interlocking forces give birth to the "Ten Thousand Things": you, me, the stars, the mountains, and the cat on my lap. Yin and yang, in continuous motion, form and underlie all those things we commonly call animate and all those we commonly call inanimate, in other words, all of worldly existence.[4]

You can trace the progression in either direction, forward or backward: Tao ➜ yin and yang ➜ Ten Thousand Things, or Ten Thousand Things ➜ yin and yang ➜ Tao. They mirror each other. We can know the mother by knowing the children, and we can know the children by knowing the mother.[5]

Laotse calls the Tao the "Eternal Law," meaning the inescapable cycle of growth and decay, life and death.[6] This is the essence of the perpetual movement of the Way—circular and always returning. Everything is generated by the Tao and everything returns to the Tao. Endings are beginnings; beginnings are endings. "Even when the body dies, it is not the end," Laotse says.[7] And "He who has Tao has all eternity."[8] The Tao exists beyond space and time.

Because all opposites eventually revert to each other, there are no distinctions within the Tao. There's no good, no evil. Emerson helps explain this in his Journal of 1838: "The fact detached is ugly. Replace it in its series of cause & effect, and it is beautiful. Putrefaction is loathsome; but putrefaction seen as a step in the circle of nature, pleases. ...The laws of disease are the laws of health unmasked."[9] Why should we recoil at the savagery of nature? We have to accept that what Emerson also calls the Law surpasses rational thought.[10] We can't even distinguish between good luck and bad luck. "One day your loss may be your fortune / one day your fortune may be your loss," Laotse tells us.[11] Emerson is even more succinct: "Evil will bless, and ice will burn."[12]

We are all subjects of the Eternal Law. Fortunately for us, because it's beyond distinctions, it's utterly nonjudgmental and infinitely forgiving. It is "the good man's treasure" and "the bad man's refuge;"[13] "the great wealth of those who are awake" and "the great protector of those still sleeping."[14] One translator echoes the Bible: "Seek and you will find / Err and you will be forgiven."[15] The Tao is with every one of us—good and bad—always. It does not withhold itself and we don't have to search for it.[16]

Emerson calls the Tao the Over-Soul. He experiences this indefinable and immeasurable "first and last reality" as subtle and quiet, yet tenacious.[17] He makes glancing contact with this vastness in conversations, daydreams, night dreams, and in times of grief or passion.[18]

Emerson writes, "This deep power in which we exist and whose beatitude is all accessible to us is not only self-sufficing and perfect in every hour, but the act of seeing and the thing seen, ...the subject and the object are one. We see the world piece by piece, as the sun, the moon, the animal, the tree; but the whole, of which these are the shining parts, is the soul."[19] I have entered this state of oneness, this loss of separate self, this fusing of subject and object so there's no observer and no observed during rare

T'ai Chi practices and while sitting.

The Tao is a mirror, or rather an infinite number of mirrors reflecting each other. "The world globes itself in a drop of dew," as Emerson puts it.[20] "Without going outside / one can know the whole world," Laotse writes.[21] The reclusive Emily Dickinson is proof of this. Each one of us contains the universe and every mundane thing we do is a metaphor for everything else—on both the material and immaterial level. All the skills my students and I hone by practicing T'ai Chi are metaphors: noticing the transfer of weight from one leg to another, focusing on what we're doing with our eyes, coordinating breath (inner) with movement (outer), and so on. While we're working on integrating all parts of our bodies, our spirits are going through the same motions, mirroring, and learning the same things whether we intend it or not.

One of the aspects of the Tao that interests me most is its neutrality. It doesn't care who wins the soccer game. Translators use the words "merciless", "ruthless," and "impartial" to describe it. I think the last conveys the proper nuance in English. It's pure energy, there for us to use—for good or ill. We can enhance our ability to tap into this energy, gather it and direct it, through practices like T'ai Chi, meditation, qigong, Yoga, and being in nature. I like the way Arthur Waley translates this: "Work it, and more comes out."[22] It's like a bellows.

But Laotse qualifies this impartiality. He says, "The way of nature is free from intimacy [favorites], / Yet it constantly stays with the good man."[23] Why would it do this? My explanation is that the "good man" is a person who lives in harmony with the Tao—someone who knows herself (knows the Tao) and is true to herself (true to the Tao). Thus its powerful, prevailing wind is at her back, helping her. See how Laotse and Emerson parallel each other here: "[If one embraces Tao,] deadly insects will not sting him / Wild beasts will not attack him / Birds of prey will not strike him."[24] And Emerson: "The good man has absolute good, which like fire turns everything to its own nature, so that you cannot do him any harm."[25]

Emerson acknowledges that nature is "no sentimentalist" and "will not mind drowning a man or a woman."[26] But he also has a well-developed theory of compensation, in which he thinks we are all "secret believers," because we have an innate need for justice.[27] "For everything you have missed you have gained something else; and for everything you gain you lose something."[28] The worst imaginable disaster brings its own gift of an expanded spirit.[29] And if nothing else, "No matter how often defeated, you are born to victory. The reward of a thing well done, is to have done it."[30]

Most people don't want the Tao to be neutral. They want the universe to be benevolent—specifically benevolent toward *them*. They wish for fair compensation for their good works and are confused and resentful when they don't get it. They wish for the universe to be in balance *within their lifetime*.

These words are from a Kaddish I attended for a thirteen-year-old boy: "Glorified and loved be the Source of Life and the world which it has created. May that source establish its harmony in our lifetime, during our days, and within the whole world, speedily and soon." Implicit is the possibility that harmony, balance, and compensation may not be established during an individual's lifetime. Not only is our time frame minuscule in relation to the time frame of the universe, time itself is a construct of the material world and is meaningless in the immaterial Tao.

Humans want to see Karma operating neatly and promptly when we or friends have earned a reward as well as when others (not necessarily ourselves) have earned a comeuppance. But the good *do* sometimes die young. Where is the silver lining for a parent who has lost a child? Emerson says that "the compensations of calamity are made apparent to the understanding also, after long intervals of time. ...The death of a dear friend, wife, brother, lover, which seemed nothing but privation, somewhat later assumes the aspect of a guide or genius; for it commonly operates revolutions in our way of life."[31] This was written before Emerson lost his beloved five-year-old son Waldo. That event did bring about a revolution in his life—it darkened his worldview.

The mother of the boy whose Kaddish I attended described an agonizing, unwelcome growth process. She had to summon courage she didn't think she had—to keep herself and her remaining family intact. The loss of her son forced an unwilling heroism on her which is building new maturity and even heightened self-esteem. She'd rather have her son back, but she reluctantly admits there has been opportunity in the crisis.

At times I've seen the "lemons from lemonade" platitude Pollyannaish. But even though a blow may stun us and lay us flat for months or even years, eventually we do have to gather up whatever lemons we have left—bruised as they may be—and make something out of them. If we don't actually die (or enter a living death in which we drain the life from all around us), we have to make a new life. Everyone grieves in her own way and on her own timeline. With resilience and flexibility, we can forge our own compensation. "Whoever is stiff and inflexible / is a disciple of death. / Whoever is soft and yielding / is a disciple of life."[32]

We harbor an instinct for justice, yet injustice and imbalance are all around us. One thing I can trust is that life isn't fair. Knowing this is a *comfort*. Although I'm responsible for plenty of the bad things that befall me, I know I'm not always responsible—there are many factors working in my life; I'm only one of them. Every piece of bad luck is not a judgment against me or a punishment for who-knows-what wrongdoing. The fact that I don't always get rewarded for my good qualities and good works doesn't mean they weren't good or worth doing. They are their own reward, and I keep doing them. I also do my best to reward others for their contributions. All any of us can do is strive to embody justice and fairness—in the present moment.

I go back and forth on the issue of the Tao's impartiality. On the one hand, this feels right to me: The idea of a neutral Tao that's pure energy that I can collect and funnel into myself and from there out to my goals and purposes. The presence of that infinite power is benevolence enough for me. And yet. There are my undeniable experiences of feeling "herded" in a direction. As if, as Kierkegaard says, "We come into this world with sealed orders." Or I'm bound to fulfill what Carolyn Myss calls "sacred contracts."

I had a dream when I was in my late twenties—one of those incandescent dreams meant to be a lesson for an entire lifetime. I was blind, but I had a guide dog. Just that vision. I was blind, but I would be guided. There have been times when I've made decisions purely on intuition, in defiance of a wall of convincing rational arguments thrown up by myself and others. And there have been times when I *tried* to take one path but got firmly placed on another by contriving circumstances, like an animal being prodded through a chute. And it turned out to be the only right path for me, the path aligned with my true self.

Emerson defines fate as the givens in our lives—our genetics and the surroundings we're born into. And he defines destiny as our choices—the direction we choose, one decision at a time, leading ideally toward self-realization. But is there something else? Something way above and beyond me that kicks in when intuition is unrecognized or unheeded? Sometimes unseen hands come out of nowhere to guide me. This is the most tantalizing mystery of all.

At first it surprised me that Laotse repeatedly describes the Tao as female: "The Door of the Mystic Female / Is the root of Heaven and Earth,"[33] for example. He also calls the Tao the "valley spirit"[34] —the valley symbolizing the receptive female or yin (while its opposite, the mountain, represents the assertive male or yang). Laotse advises being aware of the male (the white, the light), but stresses the importance of keeping to the female (the black, the dark).[35] (In the yin-yang symbol—what the Chinese call the T'ai Chi symbol—the black represents yin/female characteristics and the white yang/male characteristics.)

In addition, Laotse calls the Tao mild, bland, and unobtrusive, similar to Emerson's sense that it's subtle and quiet—all considered yin/female qualities. It's by keeping to the female that we are able to return to the "Primordial Nothingness,"[36] the "Uncarved Block"[37]–the Tao.

Seeing the Tao as more female than male seemed unbalanced to me. I thought it might reveal a subconscious reaching for a kinder, gentler way of being than the constant instability and violence of Laotse's time. But my thinking evolved and I realized this is a supremely important concept that I will explore in the final chapter of this book.

My goal is to keep one foot in the Tao while the other is in my earthly life. The simpler, less hurried, more peaceful my day is and the more consistent and prolonged my quiet, inward-turning practices are, the easier it is to do this. I'm reassured of the presence of the Tao, the Over-Soul through dreams, visions, and experiences while practicing T'ai Chi and meditation; as well as through messages received from people not present and people no longer alive—communications transcending space and time, evidencing the interconnectedness, the circularity, and the oneness of everything.

One of my most remarkable intimations of the Tao came to me decades ago during a morning meditation. I had already gone for a run, practiced T'ai Chi in the park, and bathed before sitting down to meditate. My eyes were closed. The head of a powerful woman flew at me, light brown wavy hair streaming behind her. There was a sense of terrific speed and terrific power. I was awestruck. At the same time I felt a deep, pervasive sense of familiarity: *I know this woman.* She vanished and in her place the words IPONA • IPECHTA appeared in front of me as if typed out on my Smith Corona, which is what I was writing on at the time. The names were unknown to me, so I researched them. Epona was a Celtic goddess who was worshiped from Great Britain to Eastern Europe in pre-Christian times. She was commonly represented as a white horse, but she could also appear as a black horse—yin and yang, white and black, Ipona and Ipechta. In her white incarnation she rewarded you for your good deeds; in her black incarnation she punished you for your mistakes—go with the Tao and be aided by it or go against it and suffer the consequences. As Emerson puts it, "[The Law] avails itself of our success, when we obey it, and of our ruin, when we contravene it."[38] Irish kings were crowned while standing beside a white mare, a symbolic mating with forces for prosperity and good fortune.

Carl Jung would call IPONA • IPECHTA an archetype—the image of an idea, an identity inherited from my Celtic ancestors and living in my subconscious. She is my welcoming door to the Over-Soul and the Over-Soul itself. I suspect the Tao, filtered through our various ancient roots and deeply held beliefs materializes in myriad forms to humans across the planet. The substance is the same. The form is tailored to speak individually to us. In my case it's IPONA • IPECHTA. Through my practices, I bring my presence into hers and know my transcendent self. I believe she is always with me, whether I'm conscious of her or not. Perhaps it's her unseen hands guiding me.

Emerson tells us "Our faith [in the Over-Soul] comes in moments; our vice is habitual. Yet there is a depth in those brief moments which constrains us to ascribe more reality to them than to all other experiences."[39] He notes "that shudder of awe and delight with which the individual soul always mingles with the universal soul."[40]

I agree with Laotse that whether I'm aware of it or not, "Every word reflects the universe, / every moment brings enlightenment."[41] I don't expect to be able to hold onto my oneness with the Tao always, but at least I can keep pulling myself back to it to make a peaceful haven for myself in this unpeaceful world. The Tao will always be my ultimate mystery. But I thank Stephen Mitchell for rendering Laotse in this way: "You can't know it, but you can be it, / at ease in your own life."[42]

CHAPTER ONE NOTES

1. Ralph Waldo Emerson, "Fate," in *The Annotated Emerson*, David Mikics, ed., (Cambridge, MA: The Belknap Press of Harvard University Press, 2012), p. 416.
2. Lin Yutang, transl. and ed., *The Wisdom of Laotse*, (New York: Random House Modern Library, 1948), Ch. 1, p. 41.
3. Emerson, "Circles," in *The Annotated Emerson*, p. 186.
4. Arthur Waley, transl. and ed., *The Way and Its Power: Lao Tzu's Tao Te Ching and Its Place in Chinese Thought*, (New York: Grove Press, 1958), Ch. 42, p. 195.
5. Stephen Mitchell, ed., *Tao Te Ching: A New English Version*, (New York: Harper Perennial Modern Classics, 2006) Ch. 52.
6. Lin Yutang, Ch. 16, p. 109.
7. Chang Chung-yuan, transl. and ed., *Tao: A New Way of Thinking*, (New York: Harper & Row Harper Colophon Books, 1975), Ch. 16, p. 47.
8. Jonathan Star, transl. and ed., *Tao Te Ching: The Definitive Edition*, (New York: Jeremy P. Tarcher/Penguin, 2001), Ch. 16, p. 29.
9. Emerson, Journal 1838, quoted in note #102 in "Fate," in *The Annotated Emerson*, p. 421.
10. Ibid., p. 427-8.
11. Star, Ch. 42, p. 55.
12. Emerson, "Uriel," in *The Annotated Emerson*, p. 501.
13. Mitchell, Ch. 62.
14. Star, Ch. 62, p. 75.
15. Ibid.
16. Chang, Ch. 62, p. 166.
17. Emerson, "New England Reformers," in *The Annotated Emerson*, p. 294.
18. Emerson, "The Over-Soul," in *Essays, Poems, Addresses* (New York: Walter J. Black Classics Club, 1941), p. 207-8.
19. Ibid., p. 207
20. Emerson, "Compensation," in *Essays, Poems, and Addresses*, p. 154.
21. Star, Ch. 47, p. 60.
22. Waley, Ch. 5, p. 147.

23. Chang, Ch.79, p. 205.
24. Star, Ch. 55, p. 68.
25. Emerson, "Compensation," in *Essays, Poems, and Addresses*, p. 163.
26. Emerson, "Fate," in *The Annotated Emerson*, p. 403.
27. Emerson, "New England Reformers," in *The Annotated Emerson*, p. 294.
28. Emerson, "Compensation," in *Essays, Poems, and Addresses*, p. 152.
29. Emerson, "Fate," in *The Annotated Emerson*, p. 427.
30. Emerson, "New England Reformers," in *The Annotated Emerson*, p. 294.
31. Emerson, "Compensation," in *Essays, Poems, and Addresses*, p. 168.
32. Mitchell, Ch. 76.
33. Lin Yutang, Ch. 6, p. 64.
34. Gia-fu Feng and Jane English, transl., *Tao Te Ching*, (New York: Random House Vintage Books, 1972), Ch. 6.
35. Lin Yutang, Ch. 28, p. 160.
36. Ibid.
37. Waley, Ch. 28, p. 178.
38. Emerson, "New England Reformers," in *The Annotated Emerson*, p. 294.
39. Emerson, "The Over-Soul," in *Essays, Poems, and Addresses*, p. 206.
40. Ibid., p. 215
41. Star, Ch. 32, p. 45.
42. Mitchell, Ch. 14.

TWO

TE
THE TAO INCARNATE

I'm nobody! Who are you?
Are you nobody too?
Then there's a pair of us—don't tell!
They'd banish us, you know.

How dreary to be somebody!
How public like a frog
To tell your name the livelong day
To an admiring bog!
                                    Emily Dickinson

Reading philosophy only interests me as I can apply it. I lead an examined life. Every day I watch my behavior and evaluate it. What did I do right? Wrong? Is there a mistake I need to admit to, apologize and make amends for? What should I let slide because I'm imperfect and would drive myself crazy trying to be otherwise? (While I believe the unexamined life is not worth living, I've discovered the over-examined life isn't either.) Overall, I want to learn, improve, pull myself up to a higher level, and bring myself closer to being the kind of person I admire. Laotse's and Emerson's opinions are some of the raw material I sift through, picking out the pieces I want to use to form and reform my own philosophy—my character—one day, one month, one year at a time.

I interpret Te as the Tao embodied in the life of the mature human—Laotse's Sage. Laotse uses the same words to describe the Tao as he uses to describe the Sage. Her pristine simplicity is an unclouded mirror of the Tao.

The character for Te contains three symbols or pictographs. The first means "perfect," the second "heart," and the third "action." The Sage leads a life of perfect-hearted action. Being faithful to the truth within her heart, she is the fullest expression of the Tao—expansive, nonjudgmental, and generous. She is a vessel for primordial love.

Translators argue with each other over the English equivalent of Te. Many use the word "virtue" and at least one uses "power." Surely virtue on this level cannot help but be powerful.

Yet the Sage feels "orphaned, lonely and unworthy."[1] I think she has had to cope with adversity and through this crucible has come to know her own limitations and gained compassion for the limitations of others. By knowing herself, knowing her smallness, she becomes a bigger person. A life of ease and privilege would not have produced the same result. "For sometimes things are benefited by being taken away from, / And suffer by being added to."[2] One of Laotse's paradoxes.

In the end, she knows her own value:

> *Others have more than they need, but I alone have nothing.*
> *I am a fool. Oh, yes! I am confused.*
> *Other men are clear and bright,*
> *But I alone am dim and weak.*
> *Other men are sharp and clever,*
> *But I alone am dull and stupid.*
> *Oh, I drift like the waves of the sea,*
> *Without direction, like the restless wind.*

Everyone else is busy,
But I alone am aimless and depressed.
I am different.
I am nourished by the great mother.[3]

As Chuangtse, a disciple of Laotse who wrote about 150 years later, says, "Live sincerely and plainly like the others and suffer yourself sometimes to be called a fool."[4] Most people laugh at the Tao and at the Sage. Only the superior person takes either of them seriously. "True power seems weak, / true purity seems tarnished."[5] And most people cannot recognize the Sage who is "covered with tattered clothes which conceal precious jade."[6] The Sage gives no thought to how she is perceived by others and "can't be controlled by love or by rejection…by profit or by loss…by praise or by humiliation."[7] In his journal, Emerson looks up to the person who can "empty his breast of all that is superfluous & traditional, of all dependence on the accidental, on money, on false fame, falsehood of any kind; & speak wild truth, & by manners & actions as unaffected by the weather, let him be instead of God to men, full of God, new & astonishing…"[8]

I carry two mentors within me, both examples of purely authentic human beings. I barely knew either of them. When I was a 10-year-old at summer camp I was fascinated by another girl my age. What made her so exotic was that she was utterly genuine—no artifice, no pretense, nothing hidden. She was clear. She was also very emotional and every laugh or tear was real. It didn't seem to me that this girl gave any thought to whether she was known or liked—no cool clothes, no jockeying for position in the cohort. Yet everyone instinctively revered her as I did. I knew I was not like her. Where she seemed solid, I felt flimsy. I hid behind trivial lies that I thought made me look better, but probably just caused people to distrust me. I wanted to be like that girl then and I still do. I hope we do indeed become what we admire.

My other mentor was a professor of Art History who was at the top of his profession and probably close to retirement. I admired his erudition and his warmth and accessibility. As a freshman student of his, I visited him in his office. I don't remember what my excuse was to talk with him and I don't remember the conversation other than that he offered me a chocolate and told me I was a philosophical person. Yet I vividly remember *him*. He was soft-spoken, somewhat bumbling, and shy. To my surprise, he seemed a little intimidated by me. He had built no shell, no façade. I could tell it had never crossed his mind. This professor reminded me of the girl at camp, except he had earned real status in the adult world. And it hadn't changed him. Again, I wanted to be like him. I knew it wouldn't be all that comfortable—he was soft, vulnerable, and undefended. But *real*.

These two people are my lodestars. I think of them frequently. Laotse sets a similar example. He made no claim to divinity, wanted to form no school around him, yet here we are reading him thousands of years later. These are self-less people not driven by ego. They bloom, like Emerson's rose, not to please the gardener or to compete with other roses. They just fulfill their own natures. "Why let the self go?" Laotse asks. "To keep what the soul needs."[9] From childhood, I knew the slick shells people construct over a lifetime concealed emptiness. It's the inner seed that shapes the flower.

People who have built up tough, impermeable outer shells are confined to those shells. They're no longer flexible, able to yield or grow.

> *A tree that cannot bend*
> *will crack in the wind*
> *Thus by Nature's own decree*
> *the hard and strong are defeated*
> *while the soft and gentle are triumphant*[10]

Always triumphant? Triumphant in what way? In the eyes of the world, the soft and gentle may be losers and, in the material sense, that's not unusual. But there's another kind of triumph—and reward. The Sage soars in the infinite skies of always becoming her true self, borne along on the thrilling winds of exploration and mystery.

In the eulogy for his best friend, Henry David Thoreau, Emerson notes, "No college ever offered him a diploma, or a professor's chair; no academy made him its corresponding secretary, its discoverer, or even its member. Perhaps these learned bodies feared the satire of his presence."[11] In many ways a renunciant who paid little attention to his public image, Thoreau may have been a better Taoist than Emerson. But speaking of himself, Emerson says, "My life is for itself and not for a spectacle. I much prefer that it be…genuine and equal, than that it should be glittering and unsteady."[12] He says it's not the "great men" who give the world its integrity but the "many obscure persons I myself have seen possessing gifts that excited wonder, speculation, & delight in me."[13] There are people, Emerson says, who are too great for fame and display. Like my mentors, they are *influences*.[14]

Display, boasting, self-justification, and pretense are what Laotse calls the "dregs and tumors" of human behavior.[15] "Fame or one's own self, which does one love more?"[16] "'To know when one does not know is best. / To think one knows when one does not know is dire disease.'"[17] Emerson goes one step further: "Knowledge is the knowing that we cannot know."[18] He resonated with the sixteenth-century French essayist Montaigne whose motto was "What do I know?"

The Sage does not set herself up as a guru. Repeatedly disillusioned with his heroes as he got to know them personally, Emerson came to see that the "Power" lives in no single person for long. It speaks from this person, then that person, hopping along like a bird from branch to branch.[19] "The man has never lived who can feed us ever."[20] He warns his audience, "Do not set the least value on what I do, or the least discredit on what I do not, as if I pretended to settle anything as true or false. I unsettle all things. No facts are to me sacred; none are profane; I simply experiment, an endless seeker with no Past at my back."[21]

As a teacher I've adopted a policy of never pretending to know something I don't, and teaching only what I know from experience. If I mention traditional teaching that I don't know empirically, I add that caveat. People, I've learned, are eager to latch onto a guru. It simplifies things to have someone else telling you what to do, how to think, eliminating those pesky decisions. It also gives a sense of belonging. Loyalty to a teacher springs up instinctively and feeling loyal makes us feel contained, secure. I encourage my students to have as many teachers as possible, to broaden and deepen their understanding of T'ai Chi.

There are big benefits to me from this policy. I'm never lying to students, never fudging. So I feel better about myself. And this posture keeps me open to learning from all sources—experienced students, rank beginners, other teachers, and my own practice. The drawback is that a teacher who maintains a "beginner's mind" doesn't go over well with everyone. My admitting not knowing something just diminishes me in some eyes. I weather the disrespect.

Commentators often cite humility as the foremost characteristic of Laotse's Sage. I think her humility is a by-product of authenticity—of not being afraid to know her true self. It's stark self-reflection that keeps the Sage humble. She's aware of her own knee-jerk human impulses toward egocentrism, self-aggrandizement, envy, and diminishing others. She's also aware of her impulses toward loving and supporting herself, individuals, and her community. Every experience every day gives her practice in choosing the constructive over the destructive. She teaches herself, gradually, how to be more and more loving. And her lack of artifice and pretense has a calming, healing effect on all around her. Like nourishing water, the humble Sage "fulfills even the lowest position / loves even the weakest creature."[22]

Also like water, the Sage knows how to yield. If you don't contend with people, Laotse tells us, people will not contend with you.[23] The Sage knows that opposition naturally rebounds (those equal and opposite forces operating) and injures the initiator too.[24] However:

> *Nothing in this world*
> *is as soft and yielding as water*
> *Yet for attacking the hard and the strong*
> *none can triumph so easily*[25]

T'ai Chi practitioners do Push Hands with a partner, applying measured force in order to help each other learn how to maintain balance in the face of incoming energy. This exercise teaches us how to yield (we also call it "disappearing"). If my partner pushes my shoulder and I turn at the waist so my shoulder recedes with the push, then finally there's nothing to push against and the force is dissipated. If my partner has over committed, she may now be in an unbalanced, vulnerable position—while I have stayed solid on top of my feet, simply by turning on a vertical axis. This is a useful metaphor for evading an attack and avoiding injury. Just give way. Why would I stand stock still, suffer the full force of the attack, and be pushed off my base?

Although Laotse emphasizes noncontention and tells us to "requite hatred with virtue,"[26] he is not a pacifist. He recommends that nations use weapons only in "direst necessity" and with utmost restraint, recognizing that one's "enemies are not demons."[27] An army goes to war as if going to a funeral; it stops fighting as soon as it has achieved its purpose; and when it returns home, it's met with grief and mourning because the soldiers have won by killing. There's no boasting, no celebratory dance, no spiking the football in the end zone.[28] All good advice for international war as well as our individual battles.

The first job is to choose those battles. "The good fighter does not lose his temper; / the great conqueror does not fight (on small issues)."[29] Maintaining an essentially calm, passive approach to life, Chuangtse says, will help us have reserve power so we're ready to act at the right time and in the right way.[30]

I've learned that sometimes meeting force with force is just what's needed. Well-timed, conscious confrontation can break through to new, constructive possibilities. A timely push back, a genuine outburst of anger, can serve as a much-needed reality check and course correction. It can be honest, grounded feedback to the person inciting the anger. Going berserk—being swept away by my anger—will likely be harmful to both of us. But if I'm aware of my emotions and feel they're well-founded, expressing them puts me and the other person into the light where we can see what's really going on. Unexpressed emotions take their toll against the walls of their prison and leak out in underhanded, mistargeted ways.

I developed the habit of disappearing as a child when the family arguments got loud and scary. I have an indelible image of me going through the front door, stepping off the stoop into the yard as if blown out by a blast of hot air. I was under thirteen, couldn't stop or fix anything, and couldn't bear to witness it. As an adult in more control of my life, I've had to learn when *not* to disappear. Discerning the difference is the trick. In picking my battles, I find it helps to not worry about what others are doing if it doesn't affect me or my interests. Best to just focus on what I'm doing and do the best job I can.

Nelson Mandela, as head of the African National Congress, said he was forced to take up armed struggle after the Sharpeville massacre of sixty-seven peaceful protestors because apartheid left him no other choice. He knew that without violence there would be no negotiation and without negotiation there would be no end to white domination, no hope for democracy. When apartheid was finally dismantled and he was released from prison after twenty-seven years, he did not seek vengeance. Instead he became a peacemaker and set a heroic example to the world of reconciliation. That's Laotse's Sage.

In an interview with the Dalai Lama, Paul Ekman sought the Buddhist's response to the fatal beating of an innocent teenaged boy with metal pipes by guards in a Chinese prison. To his surprise, Ekman learned that the Dalai Lama would, if he had a gun available, choose to shoot and kill the guard.[31]

Emerson believes one's deepest inner self—the soul—is not "hot and passionate…at the union or opposition of other persons. No man is its enemy. It accepts whatsoever befalls, as part of its lesson. It is a watcher more than a doer…"[32] But in the physical world he admires Thoreau, Bronson Alcott, and the French essayist Montaigne for their rebelliousness. And notes in his Journal: "A philosopher is no philosopher unless he takes lively part with the thief who picks his pocket and with the bully that insults and strikes him."[33] Emerson revered the militant abolitionist John Brown, even compared him to Jesus. When the Civil War broke out, Emerson's wife, Lydian, rejoiced and decked their porch with colorful bunting. Slavery was not going to leave American soil any other way.

Incident by incident, we decide how to respond to the slings and arrows. Do we oppose them? Do we turn the other cheek? We have to be able to do both.

Our real protection is in the stability and composure we can build by becoming one with ourselves, with the Tao. "To be insulted and not feel angry," Chuangtse says, "is the mark of one who has identified himself with the natural scheme of things."[34] That's my ideal, my challenge. But maybe not a wholly realistic one. Maybe the real goal is to be insulted, feel the hurt and anger, and then quickly find the equilibrium to combine emotion, intellect, and experience (in other words, summon the wisdom) to know whether and how to respond in order to achieve the most positive outcome.

Hard-earned wisdom inspirited and supported by an abiding intimacy with the Tao makes the Sage a natural leader. Magnetized by a love-suffused inner peace, she draws others to her.[35] People instinctively acknowledge her authority[36] and feel compelled to emulate her. Thus they "transform themselves."[37] "Who shall set a limit to the influence of a human being?" Emerson asks. Some people are capable of attracting "material and elemental powers, and where they appear, immense instrumentalities organize around them."[38] A lesser person would have to resort to coercion,[39] but the Sage remains unobtrusive, her effect like wind over grass. In the end, people think they have accomplished things on their own.[40]

Just as nature instructs us without language, the Sage "preaches the doctrine without words."[41] Chuangtse's familiar way of putting this is, "He who knows does not talk, and he who talks does not know."[42] This realization hit Emerson hard: "Cursed is preaching—the better it is, the worse. A preacher is a bully: I who have preached so much—by the help of God will never preach more."[43] The wise are content to let their actions speak for them, he says. They do not explain themselves. We communicate "without speech and above speech."[44] One subconscious genius speaks to another subconscious genius. "That which we are we shall teach, not voluntarily, but involuntarily." The tone a person takes, Emerson believes, reveals the level of that person's wisdom.[45]

"If the sage would guide the people, he must serve with humility. / If he would lead them, he must follow behind."[46] A self-effacing leader, genuinely focused on the greater good, willing to learn, and careful not to stand in the way of the people or give them reason to feel oppressed, is Laotse's ideal.

Does this humble, understated approach work? I think sometimes and sometimes not. I've watched natural leaders who are totally unpretentious and solely focused on the ideals and purposes of the group, still meet with resistance—mostly from jealous, power-hungry people who make sure to call attention to themselves if only by creating an obstruction. Not everyone wants to be the grass. And there are the people not sensitive enough to detect the wind and therefore not moved by it. They need—even prefer—being swept along by the hurricane of an ego-fueled, unqualified leader. It's common in my culture to ridicule gentleness and modesty as weakness.

My first T'ai Chi teacher, Kao Ching-hua, who learned as a girl in pre-Revolutionary China, passed on this proverb: "The best teacher is a lazy teacher." I was surprised this would come out of a culture that exalts diligence above just about everything else. Here, however, is Taoist influence—don't harass and browbeat people to get them to do something. Know when to get out of their way. It took too many years for this maxim to sink into me, but I gradually learned to butt out. For example, after presenting a new movement—talking about it, demonstrating it, and doing it with my students—it's time for me to back off and let them work with it, puzzle it out for themselves. In the end it's the only way to learn. If they're always following me, it's like going somewhere in the passenger seat, never being the driver. You won't remember how to get there on your own. I used to congratulate myself on being a good teacher when people could generally follow me through a series of movements—until I sat down and watched them try to do it on their own. Ironically, it takes self-discipline for me to fulfill the proverb. Being constantly active makes me feel I'm earning my money. Being more passive makes me wonder if I am. Also, the proverb means the students can't be lazy, and some don't like that, and don't like me for requiring them to exert themselves.

With regard to life in general, an important extension to knowing when to butt out is refraining from giving advice to friends and acquaintances. There can be exceptions—I think this is a judgment call among intimate friends and there have been times when I wished a friend *had* given me the advice she withheld—but giving advice assumes three things: that it's wanted, that the person hasn't already thought of it or tried it, and that it's right. Each one of us will learn on our own, when we're ready, and without officious interference. We watch nature and our human mentors and reach upward toward them.

Certain themes spiral through the *Tao Te Ching*, picking up nuance and heft each time they touch down. One of those themes is that the Sage doesn't need to get credit for what she does, and she doesn't stand around waiting for it. Laotse first takes up this motif in his second chapter (where he also conflates the Tao and the Sage for the first time):

> *Therefore the sage goes about doing nothing,*
> *   teaching no-talking.*
> *The ten thousand things rise and fall without cease,*
> *Creating, yet not possessing,*
> *Working, yet not taking credit.*
> *Work is done, then forgotten.*
> *Therefore it lasts forever.*[47]

Ironically, the Sage's modesty and unobtrusiveness are some of the very qualities that make her eminent. "He does not claim credit, therefore he receives credit. / He is not vain, therefore he is the best."[48]

The Sage has a conscious strategy in not claiming credit. If "'though he controls [he] does not lean, and when he has achieved his aim does not linger,' it is because he does not wish to reveal himself as better than others." Revealing herself as superior would be going against the Tao and would cause the Sage to lose power.[49]

(She can't *reveal* herself as superior. Hmm…this presupposes that she is superior and knows it. So the Sage has a very fine line to walk. She must guard against what Laotse calls the danger of overweening ego by staying authentic and never forgetting her own human frailties—by reaffirming nondifferentiation.)

Emerson has his own explanation for why Sages don't get credit. "You would compliment a coxcomb doing a good act, but you would not praise an angel. The silence that accepts merit as the most natural thing in the world, is the highest applause."[50]

I've discovered that no response at all *can* be the highest compliment, but not necessarily with the positive spin that Emerson gives it. Silence is too often a signal that a person is impressed enough to feel threatened and wants to diminish another by withholding approval. If they were less impressed, it would be easier for them to speak. I know because I have done this. I've also had the bewildering experience of being teased and resented for my good qualities. It makes more sense to be discredited for my bad qualities. Being put down for being organized, self-disciplined, punctual, and productive is exasperating and demoralizing. Personally I need *some* praise and *some* recognition to keep me going. And I suspect even angels and Sages do too.

Still, for all of us, not expecting credit is a very good policy to adopt. It saves much frustration. I can't control whether I *get* credit, but I can control whether I *give* it. Giving credit is one of my practices, like doing T'ai Chi and meditating. One of the reasons I like making a point of giving credit to others is because it feels like I'm making up for the times I have *not* been given credit. Giving credit where credit is due is a form of *justice*. It's good for the people who get credit because it reinforces them and their good work. And it's good for me because it opens me up to what that person has to offer. Denying recognition is a passive-aggressive stab, often the result of simple jealousy. It's easy to get away with because it's a sin of omission.

Sometimes giving credit takes real effort, especially when I'm indeed envious. Openly honoring another's accomplishments is a good defense against the self-defeating closing off, the craven pettiness of envy. It gives me reason to respect myself. I expand instead of shrink; I open up to learning. I can also find it difficult to give credit when I don't agree with what someone has done, but can see they're sincere and have poured themselves into the work. I acknowledge their hard work because I know how confusing and undermining it can be to work in a vacuum with no response.

As a leader, the Sage is responsive to the people. She listens to them, is moved by them—and is led by them. Because she identifies with the Tao and its child, the Ten Thousand Things, she empathizes with her fellow humans and acts toward them with compassion. Loving others is no different from loving herself. By living for others, the Sage realizes her own self.[51]

Compassion starts with listening. Or maybe listening starts with compassion. Compassion makes us listen deeply to others; listening deeply makes us compassionate. They bounce back and forth, stimulating and enlarging each other.

If I have a religion, it's deep listening. Twenty-eight years of teaching T'ai Chi trained me to genuinely listen to my students—carefully follow what they're saying; use eye contact and other body language to assure them I'm present and focused on them; give them as much time as they need to say *all* they want to say; and of course, not interrupt. Attending a workshop on deep listening brought my awareness of the importance of this way-of-being-in-the-world to a new level. And being part of a weekly group at a Unitarian Universalist Fellowship that we call Thursday Night Reflections gives me more opportunities to work on my deep listening skills. This discussion group is centered around topics like generosity, integrity, grief, and so on, but I've come to the conclusion that deep listening is the underlying, supreme topic of every gathering. Because it's not the way we're used to conversing, it can feel uncomfortable at first. Talkative people (like me) are accustomed to jumping into the fray to bestow our wisdom, experience, and advice on others. And we're knee-jerk contenders—if someone says something we disagree with, we pounce to set them straight. In a normal, free-wheeling discussion, interruptions are frequent. Even if we learn not to interrupt mid sentence, we still interrupt by speaking the instant a person finishes a sentence or pauses to take a breath or just to *think*. A moment of silence is rare.

In Reflections, we're working on changing this. I'm also trying to apply the principles of deep listening to every encounter I have with another person: Attend to what the person is saying with respect and compassion; speak only to reflect the speaker's thoughts back to them in order to assure them I'm attending or to ask a clarifying question; don't use the speaker's words as a springboard for my own chatter about myself, thus drawing the focus away from what the speaker needs to tell me; refrain from offering advice; and allow for periods of silence. (I find people say the most interesting things after being allowed some empty space in which to gather and further their thoughts.) I regress plenty of times, but when I remember to listen deeply, I come away from the encounter feeling better—about myself, the other person, and our interaction. Deep listening lets me relax, hang back, open up and let the other's words sink in. No hurry. No thrusting myself forward. A nice bonus is that I think people like me better.

Some members of the group have told me they feel "constrained" by the "formality" of deep listening. Yes, we're constrained. Yes, it feels formal. We're reining in our egos and focusing on others instead of ourselves. We use deep listening principles and pro-tocol—sometimes a talking stick to make it clear who has the floor—so we can have a respectful, caring conversation that in-cludes even the shy ones (who often have the most salient things to say if given a real opening). I've learned that if I sit back and listen in a group like Reflections, chances are someone else will say what I was burning to say—I didn't have to. That means I don't get credit for it—that's okay. Or maybe there wasn't time that evening to make my pithy contribution. That doesn't matter either. After all, I already know what I think. Why would I need to hear myself talk? If I listen to others, I can learn something.

The most important thing to me is that deep listening is transcendent. It goes way beyond the words and the topic. I may be listening to something I've heard a dozen times before from the same person. There's some reason that person needs to tell me this again. Maybe they just want my attention. I'm happy to give it to them. In so doing, I'm honoring them, myself, and all the Ten Thousand Things. The most precious gift I have to give someone is my attention. It's an expression of love.

One afternoon, during a break between T'ai Chi classes, I was listening to a student whose talk is one far-flung non sequitur after another. He's schizophrenic and on medication that makes it possible for him to function somewhat normally and occasionally connect verbally for brief spans of time. On this particular day I was very tired, wanted quiet more than anything else, and had no patience for trying to pick out an actual thread of meaning in his nonstop tangle of words. I was becoming more and more resentful and angry. At the same time I was struggling to listen and feeling guilty for not succeeding. I had a hard time maintaining eye contact, just wanted to stare off into blank space. Evidently he perceived *all* this. His next words were "Angry. People who know you personally. So they won't lock you away."

What he was saying to me couldn't have been clearer: He knew I was angry; he relies on me as someone who knows him personally—a friend who allows for and overlooks his (to me) unintelligible sentences and who cares about him and accepts him; and he's afraid that without people like me in his life, he might get locked away. Fortunately I was listening well enough to get this, and it was a stark reminder of how crucial deep listening is. Laotse says the Sage does not reject people, and they are her teachers.[52] When we listen to people we heal them, and are in turn healed.

T'ai Chi, meditation, and being in nature are ways I use to get quiet so I can listen to myself. I notice all the subtle and not-so-subtle voices of my body, mind, and spirit. I see myself sometimes as a conglomeration of little people, all raising their hands and clamoring to be heard. One by one, I turn to them. I don't ignore or contradict. This simple act of *acknowledging* can be enough to mollify, soothe, and quiet them. All the "people" feel heard and accepted. It brings me into harmony.

A corollary of listening and being attentive is being cautious. The Sage lives and leads prudently. She takes one well-considered step at a time, approaches every task as if it's difficult, and is wary of being cavalier. She doesn't promise more than she can deliver.[53]

This leads us into the famous thousand-mile-journey chapter. It's often paraphrased as "a journey of a thousand miles begins with a single step." I think we've missed the meaning here. This is not about the Nike slogan of "Just do it." Instead of saying the journey starts with a single step, Laotse actually says it begins "at one's feet."[54] So we have to give time and forethought to making sure we're standing in the right place and facing the right direction. If we launch thoughtlessly into a big venture, by the time we realize it wasn't such a good idea after all, we may have poured so much time, effort, and resources into it that it will be nearly impossible for us to turn around—we'll just keep walking in the wrong direction, compounding our error. We overlook the initial stanzas of the chapter:

> *What is recent is easy to correct.*
> *What is brittle is easy to break.*
> *What is small is easy to scatter.*
> *…Prevent trouble before it arises.*
> *Put things in order before they exist.*[55]

The Sage is capable of bold action, but only when, after cautious consideration, she feels the undertaking is worthy of her energy. And she sees it through, giving the last step as much care as the first.[56]

Emerson could see that humans have a tendency to be volatile and impulsive instead of cautious and prudent: "Our life is March weather, savage and serene in one hour."[57] But he knew that life warranted caution. "Great men, great nations, have not been boasters and buffoons, but perceivers of the terror of life, and have manned themselves to face it."[58]

Mihaly Csikszentmihalyi, a leading researcher on positive psychology, theorizes that positive thinking doesn't come naturally to humans. Negative thinking—foreseeing all the possible risks and hazards—is a survival technique. People who didn't do this were less prepared and—over the course of our evolution—less likely to survive. Now there's such an emphasis on forging pathways for positive thinking in our brains that there's danger of going overboard in the other direction. I've allowed positive thinking to lead me down some very dark tunnels. I have to be careful to recognize circumstances that *deserve* negative thinking and resist getting caught in the sunny reality-denying riptide of positive-thinking-no-matter-what. At the same time it's true I fabricate way too many unlikely, gratuitous scenarios of disaster in my imagination. Finding balance isn't easy.

The Sage inevitably walks her road alone. She is "left out" and "unattached, like one without a home."[59] Empty of ambition and purpose, she allows the Way to take her, and it inevitably takes her away from human companions. Emerson says the ever-growing, ever-changing self, rooted in nature "ruins the kingdoms of mortal friendship and love…because of the inequality between every subject and every object."[60] In his eulogy to Thoreau he writes, "It required rare decision to refuse all the accustomed paths, and keep his solitary freedom at the cost of disappointing the natural expectations of his family and friends."[61] Thoreau never married and had few friends other than Emerson and Emerson's wife and children.

We're complicated. Each of us is like a geodesic dome with many facets. Emerson thinks we can touch another human with only one point and while those points are in contact, all the other points or facets remain unused. "Their turn must also come, and the longer a particular union lasts, the more [appetite] the parts not in union acquire."[62]

Because she had so many facets, Emerson revered Margaret Fuller and thought her the best conversationalist in America. She combined a dazzling intellect with an equally developed heart. Fuller had a hard time finding friends because "she could rarely find natures sufficiently deep and magnetic."[63]

Some people are so finely wrought and sensitive, Emerson knows, that their chance of fitting into the human community is minute. "Of what use is genius, if the organ is too convex or concave, and cannot find a focal distance within the actual horizon of human life? …or if the web is too finely woven, too irritable by pleasure and pain, so that life stagnates from too much reception without due outlet?"[64] Thoreau's expectation of getting the same rigorous truth from others as he demanded from himself "made this willing hermit more solitary even than he wished."[65]

Chuangtse comments movingly on the isolation of the Sage:

The highest teachings are not accepted by the minds of the common men, and the words of wisdom are not popular, because they are overshadowed by conventional teachings. …Although I have my hopes, how can they be attained? Knowing they cannot be attained, and trying to force them on the world, only adds to the confusion. Therefore I shall leave it alone and yet when I leave it alone, who will share this sorrow with me?[66]

How do we become Sages? We build our characters brick by brick every day. We learn from our struggle, our suffering. Emerson advises, "Be a football to time & chance the more kicks the better so that you can inspect the whole game & know its uttermost law."[67] While teaching English in South Korea (a difficult and often unhappy two years), I had an important dream. I saw myself on the school playground with a shovel, digging through a great mound of earth. When I got through that mound, I was confronted by another a few feet further on. I kept digging through mound after mound. At one point I realized the shovel was a spoon. And at the same time that I was so laboriously working my way through the piles of dirt, I was feeding myself with that spoon.

We also learn from our faults. Emerson feels we should be grateful for them—they're the grains of sand that irritate the oyster and force it to produce the pearl. "Our strength grows out of our weakness."[68]

Laotse talks about character being constructed over time, gradually reaching a point where it's not easily shaken.[69] He says we grow through self-reflection, by looking back at our personal history and coming to know ourselves as objectively as possible, without the distortion or fog of ego. "He who knows others is learned; / He who knows himself is wise. / He who conquers others has power of muscles; / He who conquers himself is strong."[70]

I suspect it's not a coincidence that as I write this I'm also enmeshed in reading my old journals. I have more than thirty notebooks including a powder-blue locking diary from grade school. I intended to burn them without looking at them as part of a culling and load-lightening process that's slowly making its way from room to room and closet to closet in my home. I skimmed the first few, saving only a few poems and numinous, life-informing dreams. But then at 1980 I became hooked. The entries reveal how sketchy, selective, and skewed my memory sometimes is. And my memory reveals how equally sketchy and selective my journaling was. But from this distance, what clarity! It's piercing. Running parallel to my reading, a whole other narrative is coalescing: Who am I *now*? Who do I want to be *now*?

The answer lies not in who but *how* I want to be. I want to walk further and further into the mystery, inhabiting and being inhabited by the Tao. Through my life experiences and practices, I want to become clearer and clearer. The quieter I get and the more internally still, the more the mud settles out. Laotse points the way:

> *Can you clean the dark mirror within yourself and let nothing remain there?*
> *...Can you enter and leave the realm of Non-being and let those actions take place by themselves?*
> *Can the clear illumination radiate in all directions without your having knowledge of it?*[71]

If a person can let the Over-Soul inhabit his actions, Emerson says, it "would make our knees bend. When it breathes through his intellect, it is genius; when it breathes through his will, it is virtue; when it flows through his affection, it is love."[72]

> *The Props assist the House*
> *Until the House is built*
> *And then the Props withdraw*
> *And adequate, erect,*
> *The House support itself*
> *And cease to recollect*
> *The Auger and the Carpenter—*
> *Just such a retrospect*
> *Hath the perfected Life—*
> *A past of Plank and Nail*
> *And slowness—then the Scaffolds drop*
> *Affirming it a Soul.*
>
> *Emily Dickinson*

CHAPTER TWO NOTES

1. Lin Yutang, transl. and ed., *The Wisdom of Laotse*, (New York: Random House Modern Library, 1948), Ch. 42, p. 214.
2. Ibid.
3. Gia-fu Feng and Jane English, transl., *Tao Te Ching*, (New York: Random House Vintage Books, 1972), Ch. 20.
4. Chuangtse, quoted in Lin Yutang, Ch. 24, p. 144.
5. Stephen Mitchell, ed., *Tao Te Ching: A New English Version*, (New York: Harper Perennial Modern Classics, 2006) Ch. 41.
6. Chang Chung-yuan, transl. and ed., *Tao: A New Way of Thinking*, (New York: Harper & Row Harper Colophon Books, 1975), Ch. 70, p. 186.
7. Ursula K. Le Guin, ed. with J. P. Seaton, *Lao Tzu: Tao Te Ching* (Boston: Shambhala, 2009), Ch. 56, p. 82.
8. Ralph Waldo Emerson, Journal 1851, quoted in note #82 in "Fate," in *The Annotated Emerson*, David Mikics, ed., (Cambridge, MA: The Belknap Press of Harvard University Press, 2012), p. 414.
9. Le Guin, Ch. 7, p. 11.
10. Jonathan Star, transl. and ed., *Tao Te Ching: The Definitive Edition*, (New York: Jeremy P. Tarcher/Penguin, 2001), Ch. 76, p. 89.
11. Emerson, "Thoreau," in *The Annotated Emerson*, p. 484.
12. Emerson, "Self-Reliance," in *The Annotated Emerson*, p. 166.
13. Emerson, Journal 1834 quoted in David Mikics's Introduction to *The Annotated Emerson*, p. 16.
14. Emerson, "Divinity School Address," in *The Annotated Emerson*, p. 117.
15. Lin Yutang, Ch. 24, p. 141.
16. Lin Yutang, Ch. 44, p. 218.
17. Arthur Waley, transl. and ed., *The Way and Its Power: Lao Tzu's Tao Te Ching and Its Place in Chinese Thought*, (New York: Grove Press, 1958), Ch. 71, p. 231.
18. Emerson, "Montaigne," in *The Annotated Emerson*, p. 340.
19. Emerson, "Experience," in *The Annotated Emerson*, p. 233.
20. Emerson, "The American Scholar," in *The Annotated Emerson*, p. 88.

21. Emerson, "Circles," in *The Annotated Emerson*, p. 196.

22. Star, Ch. 78, p. 91.

23. Lin Yutang, Ch. 22, p. 134.

24. Waley, Ch. 30, p. 180.

25. Star, Ch. 78, p. 91.

26. Lin Yutang, Ch. 63, p. 282.

27. Mitchell, Ch. 31.

28. Waley, Ch. 30 and 31, p. 180-1.

29. Lin Yutang, Ch. 68, p. 293.

30. Chuangtse, quoted in Lin Yutang, Ch. 37, p. 195.

31. Paul Ekman, ed., *Emotional Awareness: Overcoming the Obstacles to Psychological Balance and Compassion, A Conversation between the Dalai Lama and Paul Ekman, Ph.D.*, (New York: Henry Holt and Company, 2008), pp. 95-6.

32. Emerson, "Nature," in *The Annotated Emerson*, p. 63.

33. Emerson, Journal 1846, quoted in note #25 in "Ode, Inscribed to W. H. Channing," in *The Annotated Emerson*, p. 511.

34. Chuangtse, quoted in Lin Yutang, Ch. 63, p. 284.

35. Feng and English, Ch. 35.

36. Lin Yutang, Ch. 32, p. 172.

37. Derek Lin, transl. and ed., Tao Te Ching: Annotated & Explained, (Woodstock, VT: Skylight Paths, 2009), Ch. 57, p. 115.

38. Emerson, "Power," in *The Annotated Emerson*, p. 429.

39. Mitchell, Ch. 38.

40. Lin Yutang, Ch. 17, p. 114.

41. Lin Yutang, Ch. 2, p. 47.

42. Chuangtse, quoted in Lin Yutang, Ch. 2, p. 54.

43. Emerson, Journal 1843, quoted in Introduction to *The Annotated Emerson*, p. 18.

44. Emerson, "Experience," in The *Annotated Emerson*, p. 241.

45. Ralph Waldo Emerson, "The Over-Soul," in *Essays, Poems, Addresses* (New York: Walter J. Black Classics Club, 1941), p. 217.

46. Feng and English, Ch. 66.

47. Feng and English, Ch. 2.

48. Chang, Ch. 22, p. 64.

49. Waley, Ch. 77, p. 237.

50. Emerson, "Divinity School Address," in *The Annotated Emerson*, p. 117.

51. Lin Yutang, Ch. 7, p. 73.

52. Lin Yutang, Ch. 27, p. 156.

53. Lin Yutang, Ch. 63, p. 282.

54. Lin Yutang, Ch. 64, p. 283.

55. Mitchell, Ch. 64.

56. Laotse, *Tao Te Ching*, Ch. 64, various translations.

57. Emerson, "Montaigne," in *The Annotated Emerson*, p. 341.

58. Emerson, "Fate," in *The Annotated Emerson*, p. 401.

59. Lin Yutang, Ch. 20, p. 128.

60. Emerson, "Experience," in *The Annotated Emerson*, p. 242.

61. Emerson, "Thoreau," in *The Annotated Emerson*, p. 471.

62. Emerson, "Experience," in *The Annotated Emerson*, p. 243.

63. Emerson, "Memoirs of Margaret Fuller Ossoli," in *The Annotated Emerson*, p. 468.

64. Emerson, "Experience," in *The Annotated Emerson*, p. 228-9.

65. Emerson, "Thoreau," in *The Annotated Emerson*, p. 487.

66. Chuangtse, quoted in Lin Yutang, Ch. 20, p. 130-1.

67. Emerson, Journal 1837, quoted in note #87, in "Fate," in *The Annotated Emerson*, p. 415.

68. Emerson, "Compensation," in *Essays, Poems, Addresses*, p. 163.

69. Lin Yutang, Ch. 54, p. 249.

70. Lin Yutang, Ch. 33, p. 176.

71. Chang, Ch. 10, p. 32-3.

72. Emerson, "The Over-Soul," in *Essays, Poems, Addresses*, p. 208.

Margaret Emerson

THREE

THE INNER GUIDE

How do I know it is so?
By this.[1]

What does Laotse mean by "this"? He means the Tao that lives inside him. We don't have to look outside ourselves for answers or to understand the world.[2] Emily Dickinson shows us that.

I want to bring myself ever closer to that inner truth. I want to knit together conscious and subconscious so that part of me isn't marching one way while another part is forging off in a different direction. Total integration with myself and therefore the Tao. If the energy of one's body, mind, and spirit are all flowing in one direction, Emerson theorizes, a person could have unlimited power.[3] But it takes courage. It takes *faith*.

Emerson challenges himself to *believe* that by holding his ear close to his soul he can always know the true way—even transcend the constant muddle of life's choices and judgment calls.[4] The Quaker elder, Mary Rotch, was a powerful model and incentive for him. Rotch's unshakable conviction that the "New Light" within her was the only religious authority—not the Bible—got her ejected from her congregation. Emerson writes in his journal that "she learned to have *no choice*, to acquiesce without understanding the reason when she found an obstruction to any particular course of action."[5] That's faith.

The Inner Guide is not just a light illuminating the way. It is an engine, a tidal force. It is enthusiasm. And, as Emerson says, nothing great was ever done without it.[6] His thinking was bolstered by the writing of a Swiss woman, Madame de Stael, who noted the etymology of the word: *en* + *theos*, or "god in us."[7]

Inspiration, revelation, genius, enthusiasm, the transcendent within us: They have the power to sweep us away. We forget ourselves; we surprise ourselves; we punch through the old envelope and *don't know why*. Emerson quotes Oliver Cromwell: "A man never rises so high as when he knows not whither he is going."[8]

Inspiration brings with it the intention, the indomitable *will* that the new truth will prevail.[9] Emerson cheerleads us on when he says, "Never mind the ridicule, never mind the defeat: up again, old heart! ...there is victory for all justice; and the true romance which the world exists to realize, will be the transformation of genius into practical power."[10] If we can merge with our inner guide, external circumstances will conform to us and augment our strength.[11]

Laotse exhorts us in chapter after chapter to adhere to the Tao and have faith in it. If we do, it will readily lend us its power.[12] "All under heaven will come / As streams and torrents flow into a great river or sea."[13] Faith, belief, identity with the Tao is essential for our lives to be harmonious and spiritually successful. There are no half measures.

> *When man identifies with achievement [of the Tao],*
>   *achievement also willingly identifies with man.*
> *When man identifies with losing [the Tao],*
>   *losing willingly identifies with man.*
> *If one does not believe enough in this identity,*
>   *then it will not take place.*[14]

Because we are the Tao, adhering to it means relying on

ourselves. We are meant to be courageous explorers, always in motion. All truth is provisional, waiting to be displaced by the next stroke of insight. "People wish to be settled: only as far as they are unsettled is there any hope for them."[15] Too much reverence for our past acts, thoughts, and words; the inability to admit that we're wrong; the reluctance to confuse or disappoint others can stifle our natural growth and metamorphosis. "A foolish consistency is the hobgoblin of little minds."[16]

Emerson knew he was part of a community—and needed to be so. But he was determined to fulfill his obligations to family, friends, and society in "a new and unprecedented way"[17] that allowed him to follow his Inner Guide as it led him along unfamiliar corridors that opened to one light-filled room after another. The heart, the soul, the Inner Guide "refuses to be imprisoned."[18]

There's no room for fear as we blast off into the void. Emerson thinks even hope is beneath the Sage.[19] Prayer to anything outside oneself is a form of begging. Ideally, prayer—to the god within us—infuses our every act.[20] And prayers to ourselves, Emerson assures us, are always answered.[21]

Yet the sudden death of Emerson's five-year-old son, Waldo, of scarlet fever in 1842 shattered his core. In his desolation, he was angry, bitter, confused, and at the same time defiant.[22] He journals, "...I am a dwarf & remain a dwarf. That is to say, I believe in Fate. As long as I am weak, I shall talk of Fate; whenever God fills me with his fullness, I shall see the disappearance of Fate. I am Defeated all the time; yet to Victory I am born."[23]

We are not easily killed. Or, rather, I think I *have* been killed many times in my life, but have also been reborn. The creative force of the Inner Guide has the power of resurrection. Emerson wondered at his capacity to re-engage in life after Waldo's death, and thought for a time that it was a sign of his inability to take hold of reality—a sign of shallowness or denial. It's just human resilience, and it astonishes.

Solon, the Athenian writer, said, "Know thyself." Emerson builds on this with "Trust thyself."[24] When he addressed the Harvard Divinity School at the age of thirty-five, he took it even further with "Obey thyself."[25] This outraged the faculty and administration—all good Unitarians—because it made gods of humans. He wasn't invited back for thirty years.

Being faithful to oneself is the only way to find peace. External circumstances wobble from good to bad and back again.[26] Only inner harmony can keep us in balance.

Emerson's eloquence shines in these words:

> As the traveler who has lost his way, throws his reins on his horse's neck, and trusts to the instincts of the animal to find his road, so must we do with the divine animal who carries us through this world.[27]

Traditional practices like T'ai Chi and meditation can test our self-reliance—because they are steeped in tradition. We revere tradition because it's the accumulation of knowledge, experience, and wisdom over a long period of time. But that accretion does not stop. Anyone who practices an art intensely over many years will inevitably have something to add to it—and should freely do so. Arbitrarily freezing a tradition at any particular stage stifles and smothers it. It becomes a dead thing and has the insidious power to deaden its practitioners.

There's more than one tributary and more than one fork in the river of tradition feeding T'ai Chi and meditation. It's not uncommon for instructors in each stream to claim that theirs is the only authentic one—none of the others are valid. My original T'ai Chi teacher, who learned as a girl in pre-Revolutionary China, claimed this. It didn't take long for me to get a broader view. I keep exploring and trying out styles and teachers. I select from each what resonates with me and incorporate it into my practice. My ways of doing T'ai Chi and meditation evolve from month to month, year to year, and decade to decade, escorted by my Inner Guide.

A potter friend of mine who worked with indigenous people in Nepal, helping to make their methods of producing ceramics more efficient and remunerative, came back to the U.S. convinced that the purpose of tradition was to keep things from changing. Change takes thought and initiative. Humans tend to be naturally inert.

I attended a Yoga retreat and sat at lunch with two other participants. One woman said that when she meditated, her arms wanted to rise upward, but she didn't let them because her guru required his devotees to keep their hands on their knees. What a shame! I told her that I had the same impulse and allowed my arms to do whatever they wanted to do. I'm always curious to see where they'll go, how high, and where and when they'll come down. This is how I learn about myself. If I were a guru, I suppose I'd make arms rising mandatory. And who knows for how long my followers would go through these motions whether they were in accord with their own inclinations or not.

Part of T'ai Chi is an exercise called Silk Reeling. It enhances the spiral flow of energy through the body. Fortunately my training has never included the direction of the spirals, so I was left to discover that for myself. This continues to be such a delightful and rewarding pursuit—to feel the energy circling one way, then reversing and going another as it rises and falls and turns my body from side to side. This is the perfect example of how my practices help me tune into myself on every level, joining conscious awareness with what are normally unconscious processes. Combining these two things sparks an alchemical reaction that generates power on a new, amplified level. Because I'm joining forces with myself.

Meditative practices give us a chance to slow down and *notice*. This is one of the ways we get to know our Inner Guide. Slavishly following a tradition or another's teaching is a good way to get pulled away from that compass; it's a great way to get lost. Tradition has to be seen as an organic, living thing. I agree with Emerson when he says no one should think that what was done in some other age by some other—possibly famous—person has any deeper validity than what she is doing right now.[28]

The more faith I have in my Inner Guide, the less curiosity and anxiety I have about the future. I used to cast the *I Ching*—the ancient Chinese *Book of Change*—when I felt stymied and unable to choose a course or wanted to divine the outcome of a decision I'd already made. I have great respect—awe even—for the *I Ching*. It's an uncannily insightful map of the inexorable patterns of change. Still, its answers are in words, which in themselves have their limitations, and these words come from outside of me and are prey to my distortions, misinterpretations, and wishful thinking.

Chuangtse wrote fanciful stories about all sorts of imaginary and real people—including himself and Laotse. He "quotes" Laotse as teaching that, among the "principles of mental hygiene," are: "Can you never forsake the Tao? Can you divine fortune and misfortune without the help of soothsayers?"[29]

I only go inside for my answers now. I don't mean that other people, other sources outside of me don't inform me and awaken me to myself. They do all the time. My interactions with people, nature, and events pull responses out of me that I hold up to the light and examine so I can know them, and through them, myself. Observing others and listening to trusted friends and counselors are all part of the process. But I never doubt that ultimately I'm on my own. And the most important "decisions" of my life can't even be called decisions. They were dictated to me by my Inner Guide, and it's left for me to figure out how I will implement them and how readily. The more I drag my feet, the more I suffer.

A few times in the past I tried to take paths that—rationally—I thought would be good for me. I had to knowingly and resolutely silence my Inner Guide in order to even look down those roads. I thought they were a way of "taking care of myself" materially and financially. Following my Inner Guide had been exhilarating and fulfilling, but hard, and exacted a frugality that I was tired of. However, road blocks appeared to stop me from taking those practical paths. At the time I felt disappointed and thwarted. It was only later—maybe years later—that I realized I'd had a lucky escape. Those choices would have betrayed my true self. It does at times feel as if there's something beyond my own intuition that guides me when I fail to detect or heed that intuition. Is it Ipona Ipechta? An expanded, collective unconscious? Or what Emerson calls the "will of all mind"?[30] Whatever its name, it does not allow me to stray for long.

My dream of many years ago used a guide dog as a metaphor for my Inner Guide. As time passes and I come into closer harmony with myself and the Tao, I seem to be a little less blind. It's not words or evolving scenarios that I see. It's the tidal movement that I'm more and more sensitive to. I know better how to go limp, let it pick me up and carry me in a *direction*. I trust it; I have faith in it. All the tiny hairs of practical details will be combed into line by its broad brush. So, immersed in the now whose strands wave gently toward the next now, I'm borne along.

Years ago I had a phone conversation with a friend who was feeling painfully anxious about her future—her health was threatened and she feared she wouldn't have time to do all she wanted to do. I caught her anxiety. Soon after our talk, I went to bed. As I was drifting off, a loving relative who was no longer alive spoke these words to me in a vision: "Don't worry about time. Humans measure time by the aging of their bodies, so they think time moves in only one direction. In reality, it moves in all directions—forward, backward, and sideways."

This was comforting. And it has all sorts of mind-blowing implications—including that time is not just circular but spherical, and there could be parallel universes. Comprehending all this is beyond my current capacity. What I can actually apply from the message is the *presence* of the past and future in the now. They're all one, and all three are with us always. There's no need to predict the future or know how much future lies in front of me. It's only for me to pay close attention to where I am now—to the ground beneath my feet.

Emerson says about our attempts to look into the future, "...the soul will not have us read any other cipher than that of cause and effect. By this veil which curtains events it instructs the children of men to live in today." "Work and live," he tells us, "...the question and the answer are one."[31]

My Inner Guide is always keen to speak to me, but I have to get quiet in order to hear it. Daily meditative practices help me empty out and make space for the Tao and its oracle. Laotse recommends Taoist Yoga—focusing on the breath "to reach harmony and become as an innocent babe."[32]

With stillness and quiet, idle and vexatious chatter gradually evaporates and—on a really good day—I lose my self and enter the realm of Non-being. I call it "going nowhere." There's no effort involved. It's the lack of trying that makes it possible—I just make myself available. My truth, my inner light, always comes out of nowhere.

One of my students told me of his own experience: He took a solo hike on his favorite trail, which led through a forest to a bluff overlooking the ocean. He stopped there and practiced a long, traditional T'ai Chi sequence. As his hands drifted downward to conclude, tears fell onto his T-shirt in big, heavy drops—"like rain," he said. Then he heard a voice: "It's okay, you belong here." Did it come from inside or outside his head? He couldn't tell. While he related this story, he kept interrupting himself to impress on me what a practical man he was—as a physician he saw human disease and suffering every day and did not consider himself a spiritual person. Yet at that moment he felt not only embraced by the universe, but "blessed." The sensation was unique—he was used to being liked and respected by grateful patients, but this went beyond that. The impulse to say thank you welled up in him. He had experienced a moment of grace; the "peace that passeth all understanding." And is this an example of the Tao staying with the good man? Certainly he reaped the fruit of becoming still and empty so that the Tao could enter.

Laotse stresses the importance of emptiness, noting it's the hollow space that makes the pot useful.[33] "You cannot rule men nor serve heaven," he tells us, "unless you have laid up a store." Laying up a store means gathering reserve energy through contemplative practices.[34]

Constant distraction and sensory overload lead to exhaustion, numbness and apathy. Ironically our answer to this is to pile on more external stimuli to try to keep ourselves entertained and escape looking at our central sadness and confusion. The voice of the Inner Guide can't be heard over the cacophony. "When there is silence / one finds peace / When there is silence / one finds the anchor of the universe within himself."[35]

I share that instinctive human impulse to clutch at distraction in order to avoid looking into the mirror. It takes courage to peer in over and over again. Sometimes my initial minutes of meditating, practicing T'ai Chi, or being alone in nature are spent crying as I confront my bottommost self. But I know from experience that I have to go through this phase to have any hope of reaching clarity. More than once, I've used intense periods—weeks, months—of meditation to pull myself out of a deep depression.

I admire Emerson's courage. He's not afraid of the mirror or of sharing what he sees there with others. He knows the Over-Soul will not make itself known to cowards.[36] "But if he would know what the great God speaketh, he must 'go into his closet and shut the door,' as Jesus said."[37] The opinions, perceptions, and expectations of others have to be shut out so one can be directed by one's unique Inner Guide. "...the question ever is, not, what you have done or forborne, but, at whose command you have done or forborne it."[38]

In his eulogy to Thoreau, Emerson marvels at how his friend "knew how to sit immovable, a part of the rock he rested on, until the bird, the reptile, the fish, which had retired from him, should come back, and resume its habits, nay, moved by curiosity, should come to him and watch him."[39] Emerson used his own daily immersion in the sacredness of nature as a way to get quiet and listen.

My T'ai Chi practice is an excuse to get outside in the mornings. And a way to stay—comfortably—in one lovely place almost no matter what the weather. The sky, the soft green earth, the trees, and the animals welcome me. I start out still and begin moving when my arms rise by themselves. This morning a doe and two spotted fawns approached to within fifteen feet and stood there staring as I completed the last ten minutes of my sequence. They were probably wondering what I was. Humans don't move in that slow, silent, continuous way. One morning I turned to see a motionless bobcat watching me from the edge of some trees a few yards away. A neighbor's dog had her own meditation practice while I did the sequence. She stood directly in front of me, transfixed, feet planted, staring unblinkingly. The moment I finished and started walking away the spell was broken. She trotted off to her daily rounds.

When I was a potter, I'd set aside a day here and there when my plan was to have no plan. I would entertain no thought of practicality—technically or in the marketplace. I only had some well-aged, well-wedged clay and my hands. This emptiness is where many of my new ideas came from.

It has not been easy making a living as a potter, T'ai Chi instructor, painter, and writer. But I followed my bliss (my Inner Guide) into these worlds and I've noticed an odd phenomenon. I call it the "loaves and fishes thing." When I looked at the numbers, it often didn't seem the work could adequately provide for me. But somehow it did. There was always (maybe just barely) enough. It feels as if the Tao has pitched in and lent me its energy because I have thrown in my lot with it.

In September of 2015 I emerged from an annual swim in my sacred Crater Lake and was struck by a thunderbolt: I was done teaching T'ai Chi sequences to people. It was cathartic. It's true my restlessness had been building, but still I was surprised. I was sixty-seven—too old for this sort of tectonic change. I thought I'd eventually drop dead during a T'ai Chi class, just as—when I was a potter—I expected to come to my end with a face plant into spinning clay. The question, "What, again? You expect me to do this again?" was loud in my head. There were the usual financial concerns and identity concerns. In the end I didn't have the courage to follow through. Instead, I compromised by cutting back on the number of classes.

The next year, while hiking Mt. Scott, which overlooks Crater Lake, the same thunderbolt found me. This time I summoned the courage to obey. I had been feeling stoppered by my teaching. Quitting would pop the cork and release me to expand. I wanted more time for my own practices—a chance to follow them into unknown territory unhindered by any self-consciousness; I wanted to get back to my painting; and work on this book was calling for longer, more continuous spans of time. I was astonished by the way energy flooded into the writing as soon as I breached the dam—obviously going where it was supposed to go.

It fascinates me how immediately after making the decision to quit, new possibilities emerged—including a three-week writing residency—and a new life started to form. I'm convinced you have to give up on one life *before* the next life will make itself known. Again, the empty space, the vacuum has to exist before anything new can materialize to fill it. Now that I'm on the other side of that decision, I wonder what was the big deal. I'm a perfect fit with my life and feel no fear of the future, only a relishing of what I'm doing and the anticipation of being able to do it again tomorrow. Until my Inner Guide tells me otherwise.

CHAPTER THREE NOTES

1. Arthur Waley, transl. and ed., *The Way and Its Power: Lao Tzu's Tao Te Ching and Its Place in Chinese Thought*, (New York: Grove Press, 1958), Ch. 57, p. 211.
2. Laotse, *Tao Te Ching*, Ch. 47, various translations.
3. Ralph Waldo Emerson, "Fate," in *The Annotated Emerson*, David Mikics, ed., (Cambridge, MA: The Belknap Press of Harvard University Press, 2012), p. 417.
4. Emerson, Journal, quoted in note #55 in "Self-Reliance," in *The Annotated Emerson*, p. 173.
5. Emerson, Journal, quoted in *Emerson: The Mind on Fire*, Robert D. Richardson, Jr., (Berkeley: University of California Press, 1995), p. 161.
6. Emerson, "Circles," in *The Annotated Emerson*, p. 198.
7. Robert D. Richardson, Jr., *Emerson: The Mind on Fire*, (Berkeley: University of California Press, 1995), p. 54.
8. Emerson, "Circles," in *The Annotated Emerson*, p. 198.
9. Emerson, "Fate," in *The Annotated Emerson*, p. 417.
10. Emerson, "Experience," in *The Annotated Emerson*, p. 247.
11. Emerson, "Nature," in *The Annotated Emerson*, p. 71.
12. Waley, Ch. 23, p. 172.
13. Waley, Ch. 32, p. 183.
14. Chang Chung-yuan, transl. and ed., *Tao: A New Way of Thinking*, (New York: Harper & Row Harper Colophon Books, 1975), Ch. 23, p. 66.
15. Emerson, "Circles," in *The Annotated Emerson*, p. 197.
16. Emerson, "Self-Reliance," in *The Annotated Emerson*, p. 168.
17. Ibid., p. 177.
18. Emerson, "Circles," in *The Annotated Emerson*, p. 189.
19. Emerson, "Self-Reliance," in *The Annotated Emerson*, p. 174-5.
20. Ibid., p. 179.
21. Emerson, "Fate," in *The Annotated Emerson*, p. 422-3.
22. Richardson, p. 358-9.
23. Emerson, Journal 1842, quoted in editor's note in "Fate," in *The Annotated Emerson*, p. 401.

24. Emerson, "Self-Reliance," in *The Annotated Emerson*, p. 162.

25. Emerson, "Divinity School Address," in *The Annotated Emerson*, p. 108.

26. Emerson, "Self-Reliance," in *The Annotated Emerson*, p. 185.

27. Emerson, "The Poet," in *The Annotated Emerson*, p. 214.

28. Emerson, "History," in *The Annotated Emerson*, p. 141.

29. Chuangtse, quoted in Lin Yutang, transl. and ed., *The Wisdom of Laotse*, (New York: Random House Modern Library, 1948), Ch. 10, p. 85.

30. Emerson, "Fate," in *The Annotated Emerson*, p. 416.

31. Emerson, "The Over-Soul," in *Essays, Poems, Addresses*, (New York: Walter J. Black Classics Club, 1941), p. 216.

32. Chang, Ch. 10, p. 32.

33. Stephen Mitchell, ed., *Tao Te Ching: A New English Version*, (New York: Harper Perennial Modern Classics, 2006) Ch. 11.

34. Waley, Ch. 59, p. 213.

35. Jonathan Star, transl. and ed., *Tao Te Ching: The Definitive Edition*, (New York: Jeremy P. Tarcher/Penguin, 2001), Ch. 37, p. 50.

36. Emerson, "The Over-Soul," in *Essays, Poems, Addresses*, p. 222.

37. Ibid.

38. Emerson, "Experience," in *The Annotated Emerson*, p. 240.

39. Emerson, "Thoreau," in *The Annotated Emerson*, p. 481.

FOUR

WU WEI

Wu Wei. I like the oscillating sound of it. Wu Wei ripples in the background of every chapter of the *Tao Te Ching*. It is stillness in movement and movement in stillness. It is action and inaction combined. My favorite translation is "effortless effort." When we're in the stream of Wu Wei, we are water coursing downhill, surrendering to gravity, taking the easy way, yet avoiding nothing, only flowing around (and incidentally, gradually penetrating the impenetrable). Taoism itself is referred to as the Watercourse Way. "The best of men is like water," Laotse says.[1]

A common translation for Wu Wei is simply the word "inaction." Although this is incomplete, I've found it can be very useful at times if taken literally. One of the most important lessons Wu Wei has for me is if I don't know what to do, do nothing. Wait. The mud will settle and the water will clear. In its own time, the level of the water will rise until it is high enough to surmount its confines. If I act before I have clarity or before enough energy builds, it will end badly. This is where hanging back, getting quiet, and observing and imitating nature come in.

Wu Wei opens me to the realization that the world is sacred; and interference fueled by arrogance, ignorance, greed, and excessive ingenuity endangers all sacredness, including my own. "There are those who will conquer the world / And make of it (what they conceive or desire). / I see that they will not succeed."[2]

I have to stop the officious, pedantic, clueless interfering with my own life. If I forsake Wu Wei, if I try to force or rush things, if I grab, I will miss it.[3] Laotse's words are a calming and centering influence: "Allow your life to unfold naturally / Know that it too is a vessel of perfection."[4] There is a time for everything—being in motion or at rest, ahead or behind, vigorous or exhausted, safe or in danger.[5] I want to accept and respect who and where I am and who and where others are at any given time in our lives.

If I want to give Wu Wei the freedom to move at will within my life, I have to be supple and stretchy. Laotse advises me to be perennially like a newborn baby who can "scream all day without getting hoarse."[6] We start off soft and elastic; we tend to become stiff and brittle as we age—like all living things.[7] Continuously welcoming Wu Wei into my life can slow this process. Being hard and unyielding makes me a disciple of death. Being tender and adaptable makes me a disciple of life.[8]

The paradox of Wu Wei is that only by surrendering to it can we hope to achieve our true goals; only by "going with the flow" can we have any mastery over our own lives.[9] And we can't successfully lead others by strong-arming them—people instinctively push back and turn away from those who meddle too much in their affairs.[10] Wu Wei combines soft with hard and strong with gentle. An army that can't retreat will be defeated. A tree that can't bend will be shattered by the wind.[11] We naturally wonder how we can be weak and powerful at the same time, even though we can see for ourselves that there is nothing weaker yet more powerful than water.[12] Laotse laments our lack of faith in the yielding, flexible approach and our inability to put it into practice.[13] It takes the same kind of courage to trust Wu Wei as it does to trust the Inner Guide and the Tao. We have to take a flying leap into the mystery behind the words, "The Tao never does, / Yet through it everything is done."[14]

Emerson was well aware of the creative power of Wu Wei. "In times when we thought ourselves indolent," he writes, "we have afterwards discovered, that much was accomplished, and much was begun in us."[15] He understood the value of living moment by moment, treating each one as the "journey's end," and finding his "only ballast" in a "respect for the present hour."[16]

One of Emerson's friends habitually looked ahead, expecting everything from the universe and was frequently disappointed when he received anything less than the best. Emerson grabbed the stick at the other end—"expecting nothing, and …always full of thanks for moderate goods."[17] As someone who prized spontaneity, (and inconsistency) he was willing to be easy-going and pliable, to put himself into the current of nature and be strong with its strength.[18]

As I've said, I've learned the hard way that forcing myself to go in a direction away from my inner nature ends in damage to my physical, mental, and spiritual health (even if I accomplish what I set out to do!). I consider my spiritual path to be the underlying reason for my existence; yet I have to approach it lightly, with Wu Wei. Too much self-discipline, too much intensity drives me off course. My recurring dream of a golden, glowing yellow bird—a symbol of my spiritual life—keeps reminding me of this. I hold the delicate animal in my hand, knowing that if I squeeze too tightly I'll kill it, and if my grip is too loose, it will escape. I have to find the middle way—one that's relaxed and at the same time acutely alert and responsive, ready to adjust to every small movement of the bird. The legendary T'ai Chi master didn't even have to wrap her fingers around the bird. As it perched on her palm, she was able to give way so sensitively to the bird's downward pressure as it attempted to launch that the bird could not lift off. A spiritual life, I think, is best pursued with this kind of delicacy and gentleness. An oblique, almost casual approach works best for me. The diversions of everyday life and my explicitly spiritual practices do not oppose each other. They reflect, stimulate, and balance each other.

T'ai Chi is the perfect corporal example of Wu Wei—effortless effort, acting without acting. I like to begin my morning practice thinking, "This is the easiest thing I'll do all day." We learn to move in a relaxed state, engaging as few muscles as possible as little as possible and as smoothly as possible. This unleashes real power—allowing qi to flow freely, unobstructed by tense muscles or joints. It's difficult for us to grasp that we can be maximally relaxed and maximally powerful at the same time. In fact, relaxation is a prerequisite for real power. Tension blocks the current of energy and cramps both mind and body so we can't respond quickly or effectively. We need only *intention*, not tension.

I use Wu Wei—the noninterference, "laissez faire" translation of it—in my T'ai Chi classes. I respect the gradual phases and stages of learning. There's an important timing element involved—a digestive process—that's innate and individual in everyone and can't be hurried. Some learn faster than others. This is not important. I let people be where they are—another application of the Chinese proverb, "The best teacher is a lazy teacher."

No one looks just like me when they do the sequence, and it would be a mistake to expect them to. They don't just have different body types and different levels of competence; they also have different personalities. It has always been interesting to me to see how each student's performance is an animated, outer portrait of their unique inner character. T'ai Chi is a set series of movements—the same ones taught by the same teacher, yet every one of my students imprints her own personality onto those movements. With the experienced students, although plenty of things are different, there may be nothing to "correct."

At its best, T'ai Chi blends the dancer and the dance. Am I doing T'ai Chi, or is T'ai Chi doing me? This is the "mystery of passivity."[19] After thirty-eight years of consistent, focused practice, T'ai Chi can feel ridiculously simple. Sometimes, when doing a demonstration I wonder, what is there to watch here? It's as if

I'm not doing anything. Laotse explains, "When accomplishment is at its utmost, / It is as if nothing is accomplished."[20] (I have a ways to go before reaching the utmost.)

The sequence is navigated while residing in my physical and spiritual center—the dan tian, located in the belly. I see this place as my umbilical cord to the universe, to the Tao. Through it, I can get beyond thought and beyond duality, past both subjectivity and objectivity. I have experienced what I suppose I could call complete fusion while doing T'ai Chi—no me, no not-me; no observer, no observed; no separation between me and all the rest of it. Taoists call this state of fusion *wu o chü wang*: "both things and myself are forgotten."[21] This is where Wu Wei leads.

Living in the slow, unforced rhythm of Wu Wei gives the Inner Guide room and time to express itself. The Sage follows the Inner Guide to join the Tao. These three concepts—Wu Wei, Inner Guide, and Tao—overlap and interpenetrate each other. Teasing them apart is a way of exposing more detail and helping us to understand them, but they are never other than all one thing.

CHAPTER FOUR NOTES

1. Lin Yutang, transl. and ed., *The Wisdom of Laotse*, (New York: Random House Modern Library, 1948), Ch. 8, p. 76.
2. Lin Yutang, Ch. 29, p. 164.
3. Chang Chung-yuan, transl. and ed., *Tao: A New Way of Thinking*, (New York: Harper & Row Harper Colophon Books, 1975), Ch. 29, p. 85.
4. Jonathan Star, transl. and ed., *Tao Te Ching: The Definitive Edition*, (New York: Jeremy P. Tarcher/Penguin, 2001), Ch. 29, p. 42.
5. Stephen Mitchell, ed., *Tao Te Ching: A New English Version*, (New York: Harper Perennial Modern Classics, 2006) Ch. 29.
6. Arthur Waley, transl. and ed., *The Way and Its Power: Lao Tzu's Tao Te Ching and Its Place in Chinese Thought*, (New York: Grove Press, 1958), Ch. 55, p. 209.
7. Star, Ch. 76, p. 89.
8. Mitchell, Ch. 76.
9. Mitchell, Ch. 48.
10. Waley, Ch. 48, p. 201.
11. Star, Ch. 76, p. 89.
12. Star, Ch. 78, p. 91.
13. Ibid.
14. Lin Yutang, Ch. 37, p. 194.
15. Ralph Waldo Emerson, "Experience," in *The Annotated Emerson*, David Mikics, ed., (Cambridge, MA: The Belknap Press of Harvard University Press, 2012), p. 225.
16. Emerson, "Experience," in *The Annotated Emerson*, p. 234.
17. Ibid., p. 235.
18. Emerson, "Power," in *The Annotated Emerson*, p. 431.
19. Chang, Ch. 6, p. 21.
20. Chang, Ch. 45, p. 125.
21. Chang, translator's commentary in Ch. 1, p. 6.

FIVE

CIRCLES

First there is the Big Circle, the all-encompassing circle, the Eternal Law of growth and decay. Nothing escapes cosmic recycling. Where does the circle begin? Where does it end? The Tao doesn't recognize beginnings and endings—destruction and creation are leveled together as one.[1]

The Tao is unchanging in that it never stops changing, never stops moving—going out and then curving back on itself, always reversing, always returning.

> *Something mysteriously formed,*
> *Born before heaven and earth.*
> *In the silence and the void,*
> *Standing alone and unchanging,*
> *Ever present and in motion.*
> ...
> *Call it Tao.*
> ...
> *Being great it flows.*
> *It flows far away.*
> *Having gone far, it returns.*[2]

Chuangtse warns us to avoid straight lines. "Do not clutter up your mind with hard and fast notions, for this would be running opposite to Tao. ...Do not follow stubbornly one course of movement, for this would be to deviate from Tao."[3]

Laotse wants me to stay away from extremes, to not stretch myself beyond my limits, to lead my life gently and unobtrusively. He preaches the "wisdom of obscurity" because "the obscure outlast the obvious."[4]

> Contraction pulls at that
>   which extends too far
> Weakness pulls at that
>   which strengthens too much
> Ruin pulls at that
>   which rises too high
> Loss pulls at life
>   when you fill it with too much stuff[5]

If I want to run with the power of the Tao instead of against it, I have to proceed slowly and cautiously enough so I can sense the very beginnings of life's turnings, keep from overshooting the curves and careening off the road into a ditch. It's possible to soften and smooth the edges of the reversals by not mindlessly staying the course until I run off course. Driving on autopilot doesn't work.

The *Tao Te Ching* itself has a circular rhythm to it as themes return again and again in different clothing, viewed from different angles. And I get the overall sense of a sphere that swells and shrinks, swells and shrinks. At times the book distills into Chapter 40's single stanza of four lines:

> Returning is the motion of the Tao.
> Yielding is the way of the Tao.
> The ten thousand things are born of being.
> Being is born of not being.[6]

At other times the *Tao Te Ching* explodes into a million concentric spheres leapfrogging over each other into infinity, encircling every minute detail of my life. I'm blown away by its rubbery shape-shifting. The sphere rebounds between having no borders to occupying no space at all. And aren't they the same thing? Turning and returning.

Emerson was thirty-eight when he published "Circles," one of this most radical—and most Taoist—essays. He opens with this: "The eye is the first circle; the horizon which it forms is the second; and throughout nature this primary figure is repeated without end."[7] He had already characterized himself as one big "transparent eyeball" in his first published essay, "Nature," five years earlier.[8] He *is* a circle.

Emerson sees the natural world, and by extension the human spirit, as an evolving series of concentric circles. Drop a pebble into a pool of water and watch the waves radiate outward. Each wave culminates in a ridge. The ridge resists the expansive push of the water in the trough behind it, but the force of the original impulse is enough to surmount that ridge and arrive at another, wider circle—the next trough. Yet another ridge forms and that one too is overrun—if the pebble's energy holds up—and so on.[9]

In this way I can expand, ring after ring, by overcoming inertia and climbing up over the ridges I form that temporarily hem me in. This is my spirit searching for its own larger and larger truth. If the strength of my attraction to truth, my yearning to grasp more and more of the mystery is strong enough, it will repeatedly overcome my laziness and rigidity. The view is ever widening. As Emerson says, "Life is a series of surprises."[10] And he thinks we have an inborn enthusiasm, an "insatiable desire" to forget our old selves, do something without knowing how or why—"in short, to draw a new circle."[11]

We know the story of the frog in the well and her idea of how big the sky is. The bird flying above the well sees a bigger sky. But there's always a larger, higher-flying bird that sees even more sky than the little bird that scolds the frog for thinking her narrow round patch is the whole sky. We are all frogs in our own wells. We can only strive to have the strength, courage, and momentum to hop from a smaller well into a larger one. And keep hopping, opening up wider and wider circles. "If the soul is quick and strong, it bursts over that boundary on all sides, and expands another orbit…"[12]

These waves penetrate downward too. "…under every deep a lower deep opens," Emerson writes.[13] Laotse calls it "Reaching from the Mystery into the Deeper Mystery."[14] Nothing is fixed or ultimately knowable. "The universe is fluid and volatile. Permanence is but a word of degrees."[15]

My potential for expansion in all directions is limitless if I tap into what Emerson calls the "eternal generator," Laotse's Tao. Emerson believes this central, inexhaustible engine "is somewhat superior to creation, superior to knowledge and thought, and contains all its circles."[16]

In a very tactile way, circles have been at the center of my life since I started throwing pots on the wheel in a high school art class. For twenty-four years I was a professional potter and spent countless hours spinning clay. Each pot grew out of moving circles, spiraling up and up. Even much of my hand-built work incorporated roundness and circles.

The meditation and T'ai Chi that I've practiced virtually daily for thirty-eight years are rooted in constant circling. Sometimes while sitting, my body subtly rotates, pivoting from the center of my abdomen. Counterclockwise is distinctly energy coming in and clockwise is energy going out. (My pagan friends say their teaching is just the opposite, but my own experience is what's true for me.) I permit my body to move while sitting—I yield to the natural impulse. I wouldn't think of resisting it, holding myself rigid according to an established tradition. This is the yielding that allows the Tao to enter, permeate, and teach me something about myself. I use my body, my self-contained state-of-the-art laboratory to explore and learn.

Clockwise or counterclockwise, the current is a slowly whirling vortex gathering and pulling energy into me or releasing it outward. More often, energy is being brought in than sent out. I don't frequently have excess; I'm more likely to need replenishing.

T'ai Chi is a reflection in the outer body of the circles and spirals operating within. And the inner body reflects the circularity of nature. All T'ai Chi movement begins with the turning of the waist. It initiates the pouring of weight from one leg to another and the direction of the torso and limbs. Much of the progress of the hands, arms, and legs through the air is the result of the circling of this biggest, strongest, most central joint—the hub of the wheel. The smaller joints are along for the ride. All movement that comes from the waist is easier, more effective, and more powerful. It means my entire body is behind what I'm doing.

The first style of T'ai Chi I learned is a southern Wu style that was taught to the aristocracy. They didn't need to defend themselves—they had others to do that for them—so the emphasis shifted away from the martial art toward mental and physical fitness and meditation. (The martial applications are still there, however, and they help inform the movements.) Of the several styles I've practiced, this Wu style remains my favorite because of its slow, subtle energy-building circularity. The waist turns and everything else turns with it. Every gesture is a circle, a half-circle, or an "s" curve (two half-circles linked, one reversing the other).

When I practice outside on grass or aggregate, the individual blades or stones appear to arrange themselves in circles. I see concentric circles, contiguous circles, and pinwheels (radiating half-circles). T'ai Chi brings me into conscious harmony with my own normally subconscious circulation and thus I'm admitted into the world of circles in my surroundings. We mirror each other, reciprocate each other. Nature gets caught up in my circles and I get caught up in hers. No separation.

At the conclusion of the sequence when I'm standing still, I'm jostled by the still-flowing currents inside and outside me. I'm reminded of when I was a kid and my friends and I would run as fast as we could in a tight circle in the shallow end of the pool, then all at once we'd switch direction so we could forge against and feel the current we'd created.

Writing too is a circle. I'm not just communicating with myself when I write. (Although that's part of it. I read it and see myself; I gain self-awareness.) But I have a primal human need to say. And not only to say, to say *to*. My words on paper and I—two points—only make a straight line. It takes a third point—the reader—to create a circle. It's as if having others read my writing completes an electrical circuit and the dammed-up voltage is released to surge round and round, delivering energy to all of us.

CHAPTER FIVE NOTES

1. Chuangtse, quoted in Lin Yutang, transl. and ed., *The Wisdom of Laotse*, (New York: Random House Modern Library, 1948), Ch. 36, p. 192.
2. Gia-fu Feng and Jane English, transl., *Tao Te Ching*, (New York: Random House Vintage Books, 1972), Ch. 25.
3. Chuangtse quoted in Lin Yutang, Ch. 36, p. 192.
4. Jonathan Star, transl. and ed., *Tao Te Ching: The Definitive Edition*, (New York: Jeremy P. Tarcher/Penguin, 2001), Ch. 36, p. 49.
5. Ibid.
6. Feng and English, Ch. 40.
7. Ralph Waldo Emerson, "Circles," in *The Annotated Emerson*, David Mikics, ed., (Cambridge, MA: The Belknap Press of Harvard University Press, 2012), p. 186.
8. Emerson, "Nature" in *The Annotated Emerson*, p. 33.
9. Emerson, "Circles," in *The Annotated Emerson*, p. 189.
10. Ibid., p. 197.
11. Ibid., p. 198.
12. Ibid., p. 189.
13. Ibid., p. 186.
14. Lin Yutang, Ch. 1, p. 42.
15. Emerson, "Circles," in *The Annotated Emerson*, p. 188.
16. Ibid., p. 196.

Margaret Emerson

SIX

ILLUSIONS

Laotse's many paradoxes are just examples of our illusions:

> *The path into the light seems dark,*
> *the path forward seems to go back,*
> *the direct path seems long,*
> *true power seems weak,*
> *true purity seems tarnished,*
> *true steadfastness seems changeable,*
> *true clarity seems obscure,*
> *the greatest art seems unsophisticated,*
> *the greatest love seems indifferent,*
> *the greatest wisdom seems childish.*[1]

True power seems weak; soft overcomes hard; nothing is more yielding than water, yet it carves canyons out of solid rock. Laotse knows we know this, so, he wonders, why can't we put it into practice?[2] Why do we pretend not to see what we see? Why do we keep behaving as if we don't see it? The school of life continually educates me to the reality of nature, of existence, and I can't help but feel reality's effects and influence. Yet even after diving deep and making my discoveries, or having reality billow up and submerge me, I tend to bob back to the surface and float there. I have to keep reminding myself of what I've learned and I have to keep re-diving.

Laotse's Sage hones her ability to maintain her focal point below the surface. Meditative practices bring an unruffled lucidity that spreads into the rest of the day. Her attention is naturally drawn to the fruit, not the flower; the firm, not the flimsy; the true, not the false. Many of life's illusions are swept aside in the process of an unrelenting quest for unvarnished reality.[3]

But illusions are stubborn because they're convenient, cherished distractions. It takes courage and stamina to keep brushing them aside so the window into reality is unsullied.

The more we cling to and divert ourselves with life's illusions, the more we fear their absence. Life without them seems like death itself—something to frantically fend off. The Sage doesn't know this fear because she's accustomed to roaming about in emptiness and is awake to its richness and unlimited possibility. She knows a place beyond illusion, a place of identification with Non-being, with the Tao.

One who has experienced this state of unity—what the Buddhists call the Great Death—has escaped the dichotomy of life and death. Shido Bunan, a seventeenth-century Chinese Buddhist master, says, "Become a dead man, remaining alive; become thoroughly dead; then do what you like, according to your own mind; all your works are then good."[4]

Laotse agrees that the Sage's emptiness, her clarity, her transparency protect her:

> [One who lives by his own truth, whose roots are in his
>   own reality]
> Walks without making footprints in this world
> Going about, he does not fear the rhinoceros or the tiger
> Entering a battlefield, he does not fear sharp weapons
> For in him the rhino can find no place to pitch his horn
> The tiger no place to fix its claw
> The soldier no place to thrust his blade

Why is this so?
Because he dwells in that place
where death cannot enter[5]

"We live amid hallucinations," Emerson says, [so] "we are not very much to blame for our bad marriages."[6] "Our eating & trading & marrying & learning are mistaken by us for ends and realities." They are merely *symbols* of the truth that lies beneath them.[7] Even at times when he thought he was sane and clear minded, a new light would break in to illuminate another veil entangling him.

We swim in an ocean of emotion. Circumstances don't give us joy; we impart joy (or any of the gamut of other emotions) to circumstances.[8] Louisa May Alcott used this selection from Emerson's essay "Experience" as an epigraph for her novel *Moods*: "Life is a train of moods like a string of beads, and as we pass through them, they prove to be many-colored lenses, which paint the world their own hue, and each shows us only what lies in its focus."[9]

Emerson says in "Illusions" that as long as even the wisest of us are going to be fooled, it's better to be fooled by virtue than by vice—be unrealistically gullible and optimistic rather than unrealistically cynical and pessimistic.[10] When it came to his fellow humans, Emerson was, at least initially, happy to be quite gullible. But he was regularly disillusioned and painfully disappointed by writers he had idolized when his only knowledge of them came from their writing. As he actually met and got to know them, he discovered that genius has its limits and isn't necessarily coupled with character.[11]

I often wish I could have known Emerson personally, been a friend of his. But would he have considered me worth knowing? He was a harsh judge. Listen to this:

> *How often must we learn this lesson? Men cease to interest*
> *us when we find their limitations. The only sin is limitation.*
> *As soon as you once come up with a man's limitations, it*
> *is all over with him. Has he talents? has he enterprises?*
> *has he knowledge? It boots not. Infinitely alluring and*
> *attractive was he to you yesterday, a great hope, a sea to*
> *swim in; now, you have found his shores, found it a pond,*
> *and you care not if you never see it again.*[12]

Who doesn't have limitations? Yet Emerson did have a number of close, longtime friends. Was he smarting from a recent disenchantment when he wrote that?

The character trait Emerson hopes to find in his heroes is absolute authenticity. Always searching for and operating out of one's own truth is "the foundation of friendship, religion, poetry, and art." We must not cheat ourselves and others by working and living for appearances.[13] Yet we often do, he says, and we resent anyone who, by living her unique barefaced reality, draws attention to our own masks and disingenuousness.[14]

Here, for me, is the most profound comment Emerson makes on illusions. He's describing an inner dynamic that I see playing out in my life as I pass through its stages, particularly the latter stages:

> *There is no virtue which is final; all are initial. The virtues*
> *of society are vices of the saint. The terror of reform is the*
> *discovery that we must cast away our virtues, or what we*
> *have always esteemed as such, into the same pit that has*
> *consumed our grosser vices. ...No love can be bound by*
> *oath or covenant to secure it against a higher love. No*
> *truth so sublime but it may be trivial tomorrow in the*
> *light of new thoughts.*[15]

We have to be alert to the death of our old beliefs, our old relationships to the world—even our most solemn vows—and ready to embrace their replacements. Until the next seismic shift.[16] The ground we stand on is always moving.

So an authentic person is constitutionally an iconoclast and may be seen by onlookers as a troublemaker or irresponsible or unsteady. She has to be able to withstand the blowback. I have been accused of being a troublemaker and of being different for the sake of being different when I was only going my own way and was surprised to learn that I had made trouble or been different. In life as in art, there are no rules. Our awareness gets bigger and bigger, encompassing more and more, like the ever-widening, radiating circles. We obliterate society's conventions as our souls unfurl.

The question for me always is, do I have the courage and the energy to keep unfurling? What if I run out of steam? Emerson calls old age "the only disease," and says its symptoms are "rest, conservatism,…inertia, not newness, not the way onward."[17] Even thus far I've done some foot dragging, some procrastinating. It takes time for me to accumulate the nerve and the critical mass necessary for major metamorphoses. But gradually I get around to them. I seem to be living long enough to make progress in becoming fully who I am, in moving through illusion after illusion to rendezvous with my true self, and know me for the first time.

Some of my friends are fond of saying the prevailing illusion of existence itself is the entire material world; only the spiritual, nonmaterial life is real. I say of course we physical beings and our physical lives are real. To deny the reality of our existence in our bodies on the material plane is to deny the existence of the spiritual world. They are inseparable; their lifeblood intermingles. Life on the physical plane is hard; and it would be nice to decide it's not real, that it doesn't *matter*, only the spiritual life matters. It's a little like believing in the Promised Land or Heaven as a respite and reward after death.

I enter the spiritual world *through* my body. I agree with Wang Xiangxai, the late standing meditation teacher, who says that we can enter the primordial void—the Tao—by paying attention to minute changes in the body. This is my experience with the super-slow motion of T'ai Chi and the quietly shimmering, hypersensitive stillness of meditation. It all starts with the body and its circling breath. I call it breathing underwater—knitting together conscious and subconscious, the Ten Thousand Things with the Tao.

It was Chuangtse who dreamt so vividly that he was a butterfly, floating from flower to flower, delighted and secure in his existence. His awakening was abrupt—he was back to being solid, heavy Chuangtse. But he couldn't be sure if he was Chuangtse who had dreamt he was a butterfly or a butterfly dreaming he was Chuangtse.[18] He was both.

Right now I'm engaged in what may be my final rematch with the prevailing illusion of my life. "Rematch" because in my experience, recognizing an illusion as an illusion does not make it go away. If it's long-lived and deep-rooted, it is dispelled in increments over years, decades. Layers of veils have to be peeled away, one after another.

I call this illusion the Overseer. From childhood, I have felt it as an outside entity, hovering far above me, looking down at the panorama of my past, present, and future. The obstinate core of the Overseer's power is my belief that it knows more than I do. By meting out rewards and punishments (mostly the latter), over every action I take or decision I make, no matter how trivial or momentous, it judges me for reading or failing to read the signs that were right in front of me, or for applying or not applying what I surely should have learned by now. Always implied in this illusion is that if I could just finally get my act together, if I could measure up to the Overseer's requirements, I would win the Prize, the "happy ending." This is what makes the illusion of the Overseer so seductive.

I've learned this: Not only is there no happy ending, there's no ending. Life simply rolls along, pressing its tracks into successive joys and sorrows. With each rotation, I respond as best I can. When I make mistakes, I try to correct them, and I try not to make more. I'm big enough and strong enough now to offer myself compassion and forgiveness, and, most importantly, to *trust* myself.

I've had to learn to disentangle genuine intuition emanating out of my Inner Guide from the stubborn illusion of the Overseer. The bogus Wizard behind the curtain is my stunted, warped self in cahoots with an equally deformed society. I have no need for a Wizard, no need for an Overseer. My real self (gradually less stunted, less warped) can bumble along on its own just fine, thank you.

What a revolutionary concept this is: *I am the only arbiter*— the only one qualified to choose my path, one self-guided step at a time. Everything begins and ends and begins with me. It's a terrific amount of responsibility, and terrifically freeing—to be throwing off that last veil, to be cutting loose of the Overseer and emerging into the wide-open, uncharted clear.

CHAPTER SIX NOTES

1. Stephen Mitchell, ed., *Tao Te Ching: A New English Version*, (New York: Harper Perennial Modern Classics, 2006) Ch. 41.
2. Laotse, *Tao Te Ching*, Ch. 78, various translations.
3. Jonathan Star, transl. and ed., *Tao Te Ching: The Definitive Edition*, (New York: Jeremy P. Tarcher/Penguin, 2001), Ch. 38, p. 51.
4. Chang Chung-yuan, transl. and ed., *Tao: A New Way of Thinking*, (New York: Harper & Row Harper Colophon Books, 1975), quoting Shido Bunan in Ch. 50, p. 138.
5. Star, Ch. 50, p. 63.
6. Ralph Waldo Emerson, "Illusions," in *The Annotated Emerson*, David Mikics, ed., (Cambridge, MA: The Belknap Press of Harvard University Press, 2012), p. 451.
7. Emerson, Journal 1850, quoted in note #29 in "Illusions," in the *Annotated Emerson*, p. 450.
8. Emerson, "Illusions," in *The Annotated Emerson*, p. 448-9.
9. Emerson, "Experience," in *The Annotated Emerson*, p. 228.
10. Emerson, "Illusions," in *The Annotated Emerson*, p. 455.
11. Emerson, "Nominalist and Realist," in *The Annotated Emerson*, p. 263.
12. Emerson, "Circles," in *The Annotated Emerson*, p. 190-1.
13. Emerson, "Illusions," in *The Annotated Emerson*, p. 454.
14. Ibid., p. 449.
15. Emerson, "Circles," in *The Annotated Emerson*, p. 195-7.
16. Ibid., p. 191.
17. Ibid., p. 197.
18. Burton Watson, *Chuang Tzu: Basic Writings*, (New York: Columbia University Press, 1996), p. 45.

SEVEN

ARE WE GOOD?

Laotse feels a reverent nostalgia for an ancient golden age that he calls the Grand Harmony. Some historians think he's referring to a time 500 years before the philosopher lived—about 1000 BCE. I think his cultural memory actually reaches back as far as 10,000 BCE, to the prehistoric goddess-centered Neolithic Age, and I'll look at that more closely in the last chapter. Regardless of the date, Laotse is "remembering" an unusual period of peace and prosperity—an oasis compared to the political chaos and continuous war that surrounded him. We can relate to his plight—he could see that intellectual and technological advances were far outstripping any moral progress.

During the Grand Harmony, however, people were more than just moral, they were naturally, unselfconsciously good. They lived in a state of innocence and nondifferentiation because they adhered to the Tao. Chuangtse describes their behavior:

> *They were upright and correct without knowing that to be so was righteous. They loved one another without knowing that to do so was benevolent. They were sincere without knowing that this was loyalty. They kept their promises without knowing that to do so was to be in good faith. They helped one another without thought of giving or receiving things. Thus, their actions left no traces, and we have no records of their affairs.*[1]

(Having no written records of their civilization is an indication that he's talking about a prehistoric time.)

According to Laotse, the rulers during the Grand Harmony ("the wise ones of old") were calm, humble, genuine, prudent, open-minded, and easy-going. They possessed wisdom so deep that it was beyond comprehension.[2]

Laotse mocks our weak attempts to compensate for our straying from the Tao. The ideals we're most proud of—morality, justice, and the rule of law—are all just proof of humanity's decline. They're a stopgap, futile shoring up of ourselves in our fall from grace. Here are the steps of our inglorious descent: We lost the Tao and tried to fill in with virtue; we lost virtue and tried to fill in with kindness; we lost kindness and tried to fill in with morality; we lost morality and resorted to empty ritual. Finally there's nothing left but the husk and we've entirely missed the fruit.[3] Our efforts to coerce ourselves and others into being good are poisoned by our self-consciousness and self-righteousness. Needing rules to be kind or just or virtuous is a sure sign that those qualities are absent. Thus we find ourselves in "the great hypocrisy."[4]

In part, this is an angry Taoist salvo against the competing Confucianists who assume we *need* all the carefully constructed rules, laws, punishments, and rigid traditions to keep us in line because it's in our nature to be greedy, selfish, and conniving. Taoists, on the other hand, believe humans are innately good and that our goodness will manifest if we are left alone to follow our true nature, which is identical with the nature of the Tao. To know oneself and obey oneself is all that's needed.[5]

What does Laotse think is responsible for our falling, step by step, away from the Tao? He names two culprits. First, overzealous interference in the people's affairs by government and second, too much knowledge—knowledge that generates restlessness and disruptive technology.[6] Meddlesome lawmakers and intellectual and scientific progress pull people away from a simple, nature-based, agrarian life in which they find real contentment—the Grand Harmony.[7]

This is Laotse's utopia: A society composed of small rural villages; no marked difference between ruler and ruled; minimal ambition and minimal competition for knowledge and power; only the simplest, most appropriate technology; weapons exist but they gather dust; no patriotic parades; no desire to travel beyond the village; people delight in simple pleasures—enjoy their food, beautify their clothing and homes, and relish their customs and rituals.[8]

In his book, *Change the Story, Change the Future*, David Korten proposes a way of life for us today that sounds a lot like Laotse's utopia—human settlements that are "self-reliant bioregional food, energy, and water sheds." "Eco-villages located in intentionally sparsely populated rural areas" focus on the restoration and sustainable management of the natural environment. More densely populated communities are car-free and designed around parks, bike paths, walkways, and gardens. The rural eco-villages offer urban visitors a place for renewal, spiritual practice, and learning about nature.[9] In the interest of survival, Korten envisions humans abandoning the ruinous "Sacred Money and Markets" path that we've been trodding for the last 5,000 years to return to the Grand Harmony of the "Sacred Life and Living Earth" path. Surely such a change would allow our capacity for good to blossom.

Even under the most Edenic conditions, Laotse knows there has to be some government, some leadership. The first requirement of a leader is to set the example by adhering to the Tao—living a harmonious life in which differences and judgments dissolve, including in regard to what are so easily seen as polar opposites—good and evil. A leader doesn't expect evil to disappear, but she believes it will lose its power to harm when there's nothing for it to oppose.[10] You can't start with rules and laws; you have to start with, and pull everything out of, an immersion in humanity's fundamental nature, which is synonymous with the Tao. A leader's job is to anchor herself and therefore the people in the Tao and align policies with it. This is the vision thing. It's also David Korten's new story.

Govern a country as you would fry small fish, Laotse advises—lightly, delicately, with minimal poking. Otherwise it falls apart.[11] Laissez-faire and benign neglect are the best approach—first, do no harm. If you demand too much of people, overtax them, interfere with their lives by imposing too many laws, deceive them, and live extravagantly at their expense, they become desperate, and desperate people become criminals. They follow the leader.[12]

Capital punishment was rife in Laotse's time. He opposed it because he could see it didn't deter criminals (their desperation made them unafraid to die), and it made murderers of the state.[13] Laotse says to leaders, "Never mind if the people are not intimidated by your authority. A Mightier Authority will deal with them in the end."[14] This sets off all sorts of echoes in Western religious tradition as well as in Emerson's belief in compensation. Translators use the words "Lord of the Slaughter"[15] and "executioner"[16] for the function of the Tao here. How does the Tao accomplish this meting out of justice? Taoists don't believe in heaven or hell, so it must come about during the criminal's earthly existence.

I couldn't help but raise an eyebrow when I read Laotse's prescription for encouraging goodness and harmony—keep people well-fed, passive, and ignorant. But that's playing fast and loose with Laotse. I should let him speak for himself:

> *Exalt not the wise,*
> > *So that the people shall not scheme and contend;*
> *Prize not rare objects,*
> > *So that the people shall not steal;*

Shut out from sight the things of desire,
   So that people's hearts shall not be disturbed.

Therefore in the government of the Sage:
   He keeps empty their hearts [of pride],
   Makes full their bellies,
   Discourages their ambitions,
   Strengthens their frames;
So that people may be innocent of knowledge and desires.[17]

Emerson may not have been able to restrain himself from interrupting here to say this sounds to him like the "maxim of the tyrant, 'If you would rule the world quietly, you must keep it amused.'"[18] One of Laotse's translators, Chang Chung-yuan, feels compelled to explain that Laotse "does not really want people to be ignorant; he merely wants them to follow the learning of unlearning"—simultaneously increasing and reducing knowledge.[19] We reduce knowledge by cultivating the state prior to all knowledge through meditation. It's a little late in the day for us to become innocent of knowledge and desires (and maybe it was just as late in Laotse's time). I think the best we can hope for, and what Laotse intended, is that we will access the Tao, the Over-Soul, the preknowledge state, and design a culture in its image of nondifferentiation and universal love.

Laotse persistently asserts that a leader can accomplish the task of at least rolling back knowledge, desire, and dogmatic ideas of humanity and justice by following Wu Wei—doing nothing, acting by not acting, simply being a compelling influence, a force of nature. Thus "the people will of themselves be transformed"; they will straighten up, prosper, and return to the state of the "Uncarved Block"[20]—they will rediscover and embrace their simple selves, their original nature, and reenter the long lost Age of Grand Harmony.

Emerson doesn't believe in any Golden Age of the past. No period in history and no person—no matter how famous—had any firmer grasp on the truth than we do today. It's part of his doctrine of self-reliance.[21] Each one of us has within us everything we need to govern ourselves.[22] And he clings to the possibility of universal human harmony in the future. If only we could have faith in our innate moral sentiment and believe in the "unity of things" (adhere to the Tao as Laotse would put it), we would not need "artificial restraints" imposed by strong-arm governments any more than the solar system needs to be told how to revolve.[23]

"The power of love, as the basis of a State, has never been tried," Emerson laments.[24] We don't need more guns; "the law of love and justice alone, can effect a clean revolution."[25] As proof, he seized on the emancipation of the slaves in the West Indies by the British. They did it on moral principles alone. No rebellion forced them to do so.[26]

Emerson's vision of the ideal human is uncannily parallel to Laotse's and equally rarefied:

> He needs no army, fort, or navy,—he loves men too well; no bribe, or feast, or palace, to draw friends to him. ... He needs no library, for he has not done thinking; no church, for he is a prophet; no statute book, for he has the lawgiver; no money, for he is value; no road, for he is at home where he is; no experience, for the life of the creator shoots through him, and looks from his eyes.[27]

Such paragons will transform the institutions they're part of and authentic goodness will rule.[28] The catch-22 is that Emerson knows no healthy, whole person would ever choose the hollow, pompous life of a politician[29] and certainly some of our leaders will have to occupy political office.

Emerson assumes government has to be there, but "the less we have, the better,—the fewer laws, and the less confided power." Ideally, the state exists to educate people to be wise, and as it succeeds, the need for the state disappears.[30] More practically, government exists "to defend the weak and the poor and the injured party; the rich and the strong can better take care of themselves."[31] He recognizes that all states are corrupt and good people will sometimes choose to disobey them—a radical statement at the time, that was amplified by Thoreau in his essay "Civil Disobedience."

Emerson watched with interest as utopian communities— Brook Farm and Fruitlands—were formed by some of his friends. He was tempted, but turned down invitations to join. He felt he couldn't contribute to a utopian community when he hadn't reached an inner utopia. And he knew that in order to do his best work, he needed to be alone.[32] I'd say these ventures failed for two main reasons: They were farming communities, but many members didn't know how to farm; and they were based on the premise that all people are basically alike and want the same things—the things that the designers wanted. Emerson knew humans contain infinite variety and he needed to be free to live and develop on his own.

Emerson thinks we're good—"in the abstract."[33] We all yearn toward truth and there is no pure evil. The doctrine that we're born sinners is a profanity against all nature.[34] What holds us back from being good in the concrete world is that we forget our oneness with the universe; we're distracted by our personal concerns and impulses; and we live in our rational minds. We can only achieve goodness by escaping these preoccupations and opening ourselves to the universal spirit that flows through us.[35]

Are we good? I look at myself; I look around me; I look at our history. I'm astonished that we can be so malicious and I'm equally astonished that we can be so loving. I'm mostly surprised that we've managed to create even temporary pockets of relative peace and prosperity.

When I lived in Portland, Oregon, I read books on the history of the city. With my head down in those books, it would seem that Portland could only be, today, a pile of smoldering wreckage. What's recorded is one long slog of violence, corruption, ignorance, prejudice, and destruction. But when I lifted my head and looked around me, I saw a green, hospitable, family-friendly city, livable as cities go. Obviously the historians missed something—a counterbalancing nurturing force operating much more quietly than the sound and fury that drew their attention. This gives me hope.

While pondering the nature of human nature, I read Martha Stout's *The Sociopath Next Door*. Psychologists define sociopathy as lacking conscience. They define conscience as "a sense of obligation ultimately based in an emotional attachment to another living creature (often but not always a human being), or to a group of human beings, or even in some cases to humanity as a whole." Conscience is "closely allied with the spectrum of emotions we call 'love.'"[36]

Stout quotes statistics that say four percent or one in twenty-five Americans are sociopaths. Yet in East Asian countries, notably China and Japan, the proportion is a fraction of what it is here—from .03 to .4 percent. Stout theorizes that, although there is a genetic role in sociopathy, the less individualistic culture—a society infused with responsibility to the community—may prevent genetically predisposed people from acting out. They are herded along in the ubiquitous current that feeds into and nourishes the group.[37]

I see elements of what's identified as sociopathic impulses cropping up here and there in myself and in most people around me. Conscience wavers. It can be eroded by physical or mental illness, fear, hormones, demonizing the "other," and obedience to authority. Stanley Milgram's famous experiments carried out between 1960 and 1963 yielded disturbing results. When a person—"the teacher"—was told to administer increasingly strong electric shocks to another person—"the learner"—for giving wrong answers to questions, sixty-five percent of the subjects punished their victims all the way up to the highest possible charge—450 volts. The subject couldn't see the victim, and no one was actually being shocked. But there were prerecorded sounds of physical distress ranging up to agonized screams and pleas for the punisher to stop. Milgram concluded, "A substantial proportion of people do what they are told to do, irrespective of the content of the act and without limitations of conscience, so long as they perceive that the command comes from legitimate authority."[38]

What about war? Are we programmed to kill other humans? According to Lt. Col. Dave Grossman, author of *On Killing: The Psychological Cost of Learning to Kill in War and Society*, military psychologists have had to devise ways to make people kill with any reliability, despite our tendency to obey authority. The majority of combatants prove to be conscientious objectors in the field—deliberately misaiming or choosing unobtrusively not to fire. These inhibitions may have less sway when fighting a war remotely, as from drones. Still, I'm encouraged by Grossman's conclusion: "Despite an unbroken tradition of violence and war, man is not by nature a killer."[39]

There's no doubt, however, that humans are a life-threatening cancer on this planet. Our sheer numbers combined with unreliable consciences, and impact-multiplying, out-of-control technology are hurtling us toward a catastrophic population collapse caused by global warming. Can we turn the Titanic? How much suffering will it take before we respond effectively? As David Korten says, we took a wrong path; we've been living the wrong story—for a long time. We can see a better path, a new story, but will enough of us take it? I can see humans reacting two different ways to the crisis. Some will take a loving, self-sacrificing, constructive, planet-centered course and others will be overtaken by fear, panic, and self-protectiveness.

Global warming brings us face to face with our mortality. Can we meet it with a new level of consciousness? Can we control and redirect our nature to preserve our planetary home and thereby our existence? Laotse professed a belief in the goodness of humans. Emerson did too, but both struggled with the contrary evidence in front of them. Humans seem to lack the humility to play their role in the workings of the Tao. Maybe if we're hit over the head hard enough, and it's not too late, we'll pull this off.

Has human civilization ever really advanced? Emerson wavers on this question. Mostly he thinks it hasn't. "The persons who make up a nation to-day, next year die, and their experience with them."[40] For everything we gain, we lose something else. We acquire "new arts and lose old instincts"—we build a coach and lose the ability to walk.[41] He likens society to a wave. Its forward movement is an optical illusion. The water that composes it is actually stationary.[42] "The march of civilization is a train of felonies," he says, yet he has faith in "a great and beneficent tendency [that] irresistibly streams." Behind everything he senses the Over-Soul, the Tao. And he advises us to "look for the permanent in the mutable and fleeting," the better to bear life's losses.[43]

I vacillate between hope and despair for us humans. All I can do is keep working to bring my outer behavior closer to the Tao within. And even if principles like morality and justice are feeble substitutes for complete oneness with the Tao and the unconscious goodness of the Grand Harmony, I'll lean my shoulder to those wheels when I can. Maybe we can fake it 'til we make it.

CHAPTER SEVEN NOTES

1. Chuangtse, quoted in Chang Chung-yuan, transl. and ed., *Tao: A New Way of Thinking*, (New York: Harper & Row Harper Colophon Books, 1975), Ch. 37, p. 105.
2. Lin Yutang, transl. and ed., *The Wisdom of Laotse*, (New York: Random House Modern Library, 1948), Ch. 15, p. 106.
3. Arthur Waley, transl. and ed., *The Way and Its Power: Lao Tzu's Tao Te Ching and Its Place in Chinese Thought*, (New York: Grove Press, 1958), Ch. 38, p. 189-90.
4. Jonathan Star, transl. and ed., *Tao Te Ching: The Definitive Edition*, (New York: Jeremy P. Tarcher/Penguin, 2001), Ch. 18, p. 31.
5. Chuangtse, quoted in Lin Yutang, Ch. 24, p. 143.
6. Laotse, *Tao Te Ching*, Ch. 57-60, various translations.
7. Lin Yutang, Ch. 65, p. 285.
8. Laotse, *Tao Te Ching*, Ch. 3, 8, 54, 57, 75, 80, various translations.
9. David C. Korten, *Change the Story, Change the Future: A Living Economy for a Living Earth*, (Oakland, CA: Berrett-Koehler, 2015), p. 85-6.
10. Stephen Mitchell, ed., *Tao Te Ching: A New English Version*, (New York: Harper Perennial Modern Classics, 2006) Ch. 60.
11. Laotse, *Tao Te Ching*, Ch. 60, various translations.
12. Arthur Waley, transl. and ed., *The Way and Its Power: Lao Tzu's Tao Te Ching and Its Place in Chinese Thought*, (New York: Grove Press, 1958), Ch. 75, p. 235.
13. Waley, Ch. 74, p. 234.
14. Waley, Ch. 72, p. 232.
15. Waley, Ch. 74, p. 234.
16. Ursula K. Le Guin, ed. with J. P. Seaton, *Lao Tzu: Tao Te Ching* (Boston: Shambhala, 2009), Ch 74, p. 107.
17. Lin Yutang, Ch. 3, p. 56.
18. Ralph Waldo Emerson, "New England Reformers," in *The Annotated Emerson*, David Mikics, ed., (Cambridge, MA: The Belknap Press of Harvard University Press, 2012), p. 287.
19. Chang Chung-yuan, transl. and ed., *Tao: A New Way of Thinking*, (New York: Harper & Row Harper Colophon Books, 1975), Ch. 3, p. 13.

20. Waley, Ch. 57, p. 211.
21. Emerson, "History," in *The Annotated Emerson*, p. 141.
22. Emerson, Journal 1833, quoted in note #69 in "Self-Reliance," in *The Annotated Emerson*, p. 178.
23. Emerson, "Politics," in *The Annotated Emerson*, p. 261.
24. Ibid., p. 260.
25. Emerson, "Stonehenge," in *The Annotated Emerson*, p. 392.
26. Emerson, "An Address…on…the Anniversary of the Emancipation of the Negroes in the British West Indies," in *The Annotated Emerson*, p. 296-325.
27. Emerson, "Politics," in *The Annotated Emerson*, p. 259.
28. Ibid., p. 252.
29. Ibid., p. 260.
30. Ibid., p. 258-9.
31. Emerson, "An Address…on…the Anniversary of the Emancipation of the Negroes in the British West Indies," in *The Annotated Emerson*, p. 317.
32. Emerson, "New England Reformers," in *The Annotated Emerson*, p. 284.
33. Emerson, "Literary Ethics," in *The Annotated Emerson*, p. 125.
34. Emerson, "New England Reformers," in *The Annotated Emerson*, p. 292.
35. Emerson, "Literary Ethics," in *The Annotated Emerson*, p. 125-6.
36. Martha Stout, Ph.D., *The Sociopath Next Door*, (New York: Broadway Books, 2005), p. 25.
37. Stout, p. 9 and 136.
38. Stanley Milgram, quoted in Stout, p. 63.
39. Lt. Col. Dave Grossman, quoted in Stout, p. 66.
40. Emerson, "Self-Reliance," in *The Annotated Emerson*, p. 184.
41. Ibid., p. 182.
42. Ibid., p. 184.
43. Emerson, "Montaigne," in *The Annotated Emerson*, p. 346-7.

EIGHT

FRIENDSHIP

Waldo and I are more interested in talking about friendship than Laotse. Laotse's words are mostly directed toward the Sage—someone who sets her sights on the Tao and is pulled along on a path leading away from general humanity. Most people see Laotse's teachings as "different," "beyond compare,"[1] and "folly"[2]; only a few are able to grasp it and put it to use. So the Sage feels more at home in the Tao than she does in the human community. She's not a hermit—she's actively enmeshed in the lives of her fellow humans, but more as a leader and example than a personal friend. Although Laotse emphasizes that the Sage is humble and doesn't discriminate among people or withhold her compassionate attention from anyone, he clearly sees the Sage as someone apart. She holds a bigger picture than most and unobtrusively guides others to act in harmony with that big picture. Chuangtse tells us that nature steps in to befriend these loners: "He who cultivates his real self grasps eternity in presence. When he grasps eternity, human elements fall away from him, but nature comes to his assistance."[3]

Like most people I know, Emerson and I feed on the renewing vitality of nature too, but we continue to look to our own species for sustenance. We want and need to belong. I suspect even Laotse's Sage never completely sheds that need.

In his essay on friendship, Emerson exalts it, saying genuine friends "make the sweetness of life,"[4] and "are the solidest thing we know,"[5] a source of peace and joy. They enliven and bring out the best in him. He may be dull, stupid, and inarticulate in the company of people he can't resonate with, but he regains his genius and his tongue with people he admires and who fascinate him—he rises to meet them at their level.[6]

But for all the elevating quotations that are cherry-picked from Emerson's writing, he never sugarcoats anything. He examines his subjects from all sides and friendship is no exception. I can't help but wonder what Emerson's friends thought when they sat at home reading "Friendship" and came upon this: "I do then with my friends as I do with my books. I would have them where I can find them, but I seldom use them."[7] I think I would question how many times I'd shown up at his door when he preferred I'd stayed on the shelf.

We know that most if not all of the people he idealized from a distance were a source of sharp disillusionment to him in person: "Almost all people descend to meet. …What a perpetual disappointment is actual society, even of the virtuous and the gifted!"[8] (I can feel those friends of his wincing again.)

His requirements of friends verge on the superhuman:

> *The higher the style we demand of friendship, of course the less easy to establish it with flesh and blood. We walk alone in the world. Friends such as we desire are dreams and fables. But a sublime hope cheers ever the faithful heart that elsewhere, in other regions of the universal power, souls are now acting, enduring, and daring which can love us and which we can love. …Only be admonished by what you already see not to strike leagues of friendship with cheap persons, where no friendship can be. Our impatience betrays us into rash and foolish alliances which no god attends. By persisting in your path, though you forfeit the little you gain the great. You demonstrate yourself, so*

as to put yourself out of the reach of false relations, and
you draw to you the first-born of the world—those rare
pilgrims whereof only one or two wander in nature at
once and before whom the vulgar great show as specters
and shadows merely.[9]

High-flown aspirations aside, herein (and elsewhere in "Friendship") is practical advice for us in our friend-making. Don't rush in; be patient and discerning; know that a real friendship takes time to develop—you have to show yourselves to each other through shared experience. Deliberately choose your friends. Reach upward to befriend people you see as your superiors and strive to match them rather than being cowardly and shrinking away.[10] Conversely, you have an obligation to yourself to avoid some people: "...if those seek you, whom you do not seek, hold them stiffly to their rightful claims. Give them your conversation; be to them a teacher,...but admit them never into any infringement on your hours; ...be their priest not their companion..."[11]

Whole, self-realized people take pride in their friends' accomplishments as if they were their own.[12] They are able to give their friends room to grow and not only tolerate but welcome disagreement. Real friends don't need to humor each other. "Better be a nettle in the side of your friend than his echo. The condition which high friendship demands is the ability to do without it."[13] (A Jewish proverb says that a friend to everyone is a friend to no one.) Emerson's faith in compensation is operating when he claims that for every friend lost for truth, a better friend is gained.[14]

The two equally necessary attributes of friendship for Emerson are truth and tenderness. Truth means that with his friend he need not dissemble or edit his thoughts or feelings—"Before him I may think aloud."[15] Trust is implied here and that word is one of the concluding ones in "Friendship." Beyond truth, what more, he asks, can one person offer another than tenderness? The ultimate purpose of friendship is "for aid and comfort through all the relations and passages of life and death."[16]

The best friendship is transcendent. It does not depend on the exchange of goods and favors. "I will receive from [my friends] not what they have but what they are. They shall give me that which properly they cannot give but which emanates from them."[17]

For Emerson, "the practice and consummation of friendship" is conversation. At its best, it must be one-to-one, and those two people must be alone together. "Two may talk and one may hear, but three cannot take part in a conversation of the most sincere and searching sort."[18] Talking and listening with another human being was lifeblood to Emerson.

He chose to live in Concord, not Boston, with the idea that friends—his community—would come to him. They did. And fortunately for him, they also went away. Living rurally, close to nature, he was better able to juggle his alternating, competing needs for companionship and solitude.[19] Time alone allowed him to recuperate, heal, and gestate and refine his own ideas. It was a delicate balance. "I chide society, I embrace solitude, and yet I am not so ungrateful as not to see the wise, the lovely and the noble-minded, as from time to time pass my gate."[20]

Thoreau not only passed his gate but also lived on Emerson's property and in his home for months at a time. They could think aloud with each other. One of those thoughts is recorded in Emerson's journal of 1851: "We stated over and over again, to sadness, almost, the Eternal loneliness...how insular & pathetically solitary, are all the people we know!"[21] Emerson was lucky to have his solidest thing in Thoreau. In his last years, his memory fading, Waldo would ask Lidian, "What was the name of my best friend?" "Henry Thoreau," she'd reply. "Oh, yes, Henry Thoreau."

"Best" friendship is rare in my life too. I feel fortunate to have experienced it a few times. My changing self and changing location have dimmed some of those, not all of them. Two of my current friends, who are with me always, are dead. Just remembering we loved each other and had that vibrant bond is sustaining.

Friends cushion life's blows, help me regain my balance, give me perspective, and provide a chance to laugh at the absurdities of life. With a "best friend," I can share both intellect and emotion—express my real self, intricately and intimately. One of the most precious gifts is having a shared angle and level of insight, so there's no need to explain, and a conversation can be conducted in what to an outsider would sound like incomprehensible shorthand. The difference in my life between times when I've not had an intimate friend and times when I have is like night and day. A real friend can transform my outlook on life and make the difference between feeling like a foreigner and feeling like I belong here.

My need for heartfelt, genuine conversation on topics that don't often come up in casual conversation is the reason for this book. It's a chance to think aloud with Laotse and Waldo. I belong to the Humboldt Unitarian Universalist Fellowship because it puts me among people for whom looking at the inner workings and meanings of life is routine. For selfish reasons, I facilitate a weekly group there called Thursday Night Reflections. We discuss topics like courage, wilderness, tolerance, anger, and friendship. The gatherings help satisfy a hunger in me. And I'm building my capacity to be a good friend because we practice—and are gradually getting better at—really listening to each other.

I'm afraid human nature itself harbors an insidious impediment to friendship. Who hasn't suffered the pain of envy? If we act on it, it's the crabs in the bucket syndrome—tugging on the leg of the one lifting itself out, pulling it back down to everyone else's level and into the shared prison. Envy diminishes everyone—its perpetrators and its victims. We can only be awake to it and counteract it when it rears up. As we become stronger, envy becomes weaker. Only a mature person can be a true friend who is authentically and consistently kind. As Oscar Wilde says, "Anybody can sympathize with the sufferings of a friend, but it requires a very fine nature to sympathize with a friend's success." Pity and sympathy can even be weapons eagerly employed. A friend's failure doesn't jeopardize one's sense of worth; a friend's success might.

I came across this interesting comment on what makes people gravitate to certain companions in Charles Dickens's *Martin Chuzzlewit:*

> *And indeed it may be observed of this friendship, such as it was, that it had within it more likely materials of endurance than many a sworn brotherhood that had been rich in promise; for so long as the one party found a pleasure in patronising, and the other in being patronised (which was the very essence of their respective characters), it was...the least probable that the twin demons, Envy and Pride, would arise between them. So in many cases of friendship, or what passes for it, the old axiom is reversed, and like clings to unlike more than to like.*

Many friendships don't bear close scrutiny. As in Dickens's example, they may just be interlocking neuroses. I've noticed people shy away from scrutinizing their friendships—it would inevitably reduce their number. Being selective can mean spending a lot of time alone. We have a right to expect respect, attention, and sincere well-wishing from our friends, through both our successes and our failures.

Most of my friendships have been made gradually. Sometimes in fits and starts. I marvel at people who say they can assess a person's character instantly on first meeting. My first impressions— both favorable and unfavorable—are proven wrong again and again. I've been instantly drawn to people who I later discovered

I did not want as friends; I've been initially indifferent to or even repelled by people who I later came to love and value highly. I feel lucky that I've known some very forgiving people who have allowed me inside their circle even after really graceless behavior on my part. I'm grateful for second chances.

Animals—my dear cats (Piglet in particular, a true anam cara) and Abraham, a remarkable dog that belonged to a friend—have provided deep connection with another being, including tenderness and touch. But I also need my own species, people I can talk to on a core level. A friend who was homesteading and largely isolated in the 60s told me that although she loved her cats, she came to resent them for not being able to talk to her. I know my essence is so beyond words. Yet I need them—the exchange of sincere words that spring from each other's soul. Words are not the only way to forge bonds with my fellow humans, but they go a long way to keep me from feeling alone.

Nature does indeed come to the assistance not only of Sages but to me as well. I made a conscious choice to live in a smaller town with access to ocean, mountains, redwoods, and cool, wet green. My outdoor T'ai Chi in the mornings, my forest and beach hikes open me up to an unstrained generosity.

I've regarded Crater Lake as my partner since my initial visit in 2001. It was love at first sight. I strive to bring myself up to its level, to become a worthy companion. I didn't know this at first, but each encounter is a vision quest.

In the last years, the number of visitors to the park has mushroomed (I blame Ken Burns). It's being trampled by swarms of people, many of whom travel from across the country in gas-guzzling behemoths. The park is suffering the effects of their noise and air pollution. Added to that, global warming is degrading the forest and the lake. On my last visit, both the park and I were in trouble, essentially for the same reason—the narcissistic rapaciousness of humans.

I realize now that Crater Lake National Park needs my help just as it has helped me. Instead of going there twice a year, I'll go only once. One less human, one less car. The money I would have spent on that second trip I'll donate to the Friends of Crater Lake.

Emerson had no idea we could run out of nature. He views it as inexhaustible—a commodity that "receives the dominion of man as meekly as the ass on which the Saviour rode" and "offers all its kingdoms to man as the raw material which he may mould into what is useful."[22] But Laotse foresees what can happen when we fail to recognize that nature is not for us to dominate. Trying to dominate nature is the same as trying to dominate the Tao. Defiling it and tearing out its resources piece by piece defiles and tears us apart as well:

> *When man interferes with the Tao,*
> *the sky becomes filthy,*
> *the earth becomes depleted,*
> *the equilibrium crumbles,*
> *creatures become extinct.*[23]

Emerson and I share the tug and pull between our equally deep-seated needs for solitude and companionship. It's one of life's dilemmas. I can come across as unfriendly; I can make *myself* wince. Sometimes my "plans" that prevent me from getting together with a friend are plans to stay home and be quiet.

One of the most significant dreams of my life, which came to me in my early thirties, showed me climbing a mountain with two companions. They wanted to turn back when they saw a ferocious wild boar charging along a trail above us. I could see that our path would not intersect with the boar's—we were safe—and tried to persuade them to keep going, but without success. Their fear won out, and they fell back. I pressed on alone and finally arrived at the summit where there was a niche in the side of the mountain. In that niche, occupying most of the space, was an imposing wooden chair with a high back that, judging from the fresh wood shavings littering the ground, was newly carved. Etched in the back of the chair was a symbol that looked like a full, rounded pine tree with upward-reaching branches and a pointed top. Or an artichoke. Or a lotus. Under the image were these words: "This symbol be seen." Standing beside the chair, I remember thinking that I was glad I'd gotten to the top of the mountain, but I hadn't intended to be there alone. So there was a sense of accomplishment mixed with sadness.

I told two friends about the dream, and drew the image on a paper napkin while we were sitting at their kitchen table. The woman said, "Oh, I carved that symbol when I took a wood-working class, and I have it upstairs." She got up to look for it. In the meantime, her husband told me he was certain she'd never be able to find it. Within seconds she was back down with the carving. So the symbol was indeed seen—and carved in wood. Every time I look at it on my dresser, I'm reminded of that dream and challenged to understand it in a new way with each passing year.

I believe in interpreting dreams from more than one perspective, including that we are every being and object in the dream. So my companions were parts of myself that I left behind as I forged onward. But the dream can also be interpreted, I think, as my leaving human companions behind while I'm compelled to pursue my unique inner journey. Solitude wins out.

I have come to think of solitude as my beloved companion—its joys, its pain, and its inevitable loneliness. I've come to accept that what I comprehend, and *become* through my solitude cannot be shared with anyone. Still, I have much in common with some other humans and want to build, day by day, the love between us. I need to give love as much as I need to receive it. Friends are one of the necessities of life—like food and water and air and sleep. And solitude.

CHAPTER EIGHT NOTES

1. Gia-fu Feng and Jane English, transl., *Tao Te Ching*, (New York: Random House Vintage Books, 1972), Ch. 67.
2. Lin Yutang, transl. and ed., *The Wisdom of Laotse*, (New York: Random House Modern Library, 1948), Ch. 67, p. 291.
3. Chuangtse quoted in Chang Chung-yuan, transl. and ed., *Tao: A New Way of Thinking*, (New York: Harper & Row Harper Colophon Books, 1975), Ch. 10, p. 34.
4. Ralph Waldo Emerson, "Friendship," in *Essays, Poems, Addresses* (New York: Walter J. Black Classics Club, 1941), p. 188.
5. Ibid., p. 194.
6. Ibid., p. 198.
7. Ibid., p. 202.
8. Ibid., p. 193.
8. Ibid., p. 201.
10. Ibid., p. 193.
11. Ralph Waldo Emerson, Journal 1836, quoted in note #83 in "Experience," in *The Annotated Emerson*, David Mikics, ed., (Cambridge, MA: The Belknap Press of Harvard University Press, 2012), p. 245.
12. Emerson, "Friendship," in *Essays, Poems, Addresses*, p. 190.
13. Ibid., p. 198.
14. Emerson, "Circles," in *The Annotated Emerson*, p. 190.
15. Emerson, "Friendship," in *Essays, Poems, Addresses*, p. 195.
16. Ibid., p. 197.
17. Ibid., p. 203.
18. Ibid., p. 197.
19. Ibid., p. 192.
20. Ibid., p. 189.
21. Emerson, Journal 1851, quoted in note #81 in "Thoreau," in *The Annotated Emerson*, p.487.
22. Emerson, "Nature," in *The Annotated Emerson*, p. 50.
23. Stephen Mitchell, ed., *Tao Te Ching: A New English Version*, (New York: Harper Perennial Modern Classics, 2006) Ch. 39.

NINE

THREE TREASURES

I have Three Treasures;
Guard them and keep them safe:
    The first is Love.
    The second is, Never too much.
    The third is, Never be the first in the world.
Through Love, one has no fear;
Through not doing too much, one has amplitude (of
    reserve power);
Through not presuming to be the first in the world,
    One can develop one's talent and let it mature.

If one forsakes love and fearlessness,
    forsakes restraint and reserve power,
    forsakes following behind and rushes in front,
He is doomed!

For love is victorious in attack,
    And invulnerable in defense.
Heaven arms with love
    Those it would not see destroyed.[1]

One of the most riveting exchanges that Laotse, Waldo, and I enjoyed centered on the Three Treasures that Laotse prizes above all others. They must, he says, be guarded and kept safe.

The first is love; the second is don't overextend; and the third is don't try to be first.

Love. Acknowledging love as primary is familiar to Westerners. It's the Golden Rule—treat others as we would like to be treated. And more and more we're grasping the fact that this sentiment has to extend to everything on the planet. There may not be a global *consensus* that the concept, the force, the experience of love is the most precious thing in the universe and the most worthy of being nourished, but I think it would win a democratic election.

The meaning of the character Laotse chooses to represent this principle, *tz'u*, reaches behind and beyond any ordinary concept of love with its various gradations and distinctions. This is the ideal—the primordial *source* of all love and compassion. As Laotse's translator Chang Chung-yuan comments, "It is intuitively and unconsciously arrived at and nothing, good or evil, is distinguished…subject and object are totally and immediately interfused and the self is transformed into selflessness."[2] To lose my *self*. To dissolve into something beyond time and space while every identifiable thing or idea dissolves with me. A state I aspire to and have even briefly glimpsed at times, but it's not easy to hold onto. Life is a bumpy road and full of distractions.

Well into my forties, my experience made me doubt the importance of love, the power of its influence, but I get it now. To the extent that things hold together at all, love is the glue that keeps them from flying apart. It's also the lubricant that prevents life's frictions from completely wearing us away (or at least it slows the process). Love overrides; love transcends.

On the spiritual plane, love is another word for Tao—the empty vessel whose bounty is never exhausted, the sphere whose center is everywhere and circumference nowhere, the Over-Soul, and what Emerson also calls the "common heart."[3] On the physical plane, love is the emotional and active manifestation of Tao. I've come to understand that reciprocity—the duality of getting and giving love—is meaningless. Love is simply present. It's so ubiquitous that it shows itself even in the most hostile, hateful circumstances. Love is simultaneously gentle and unconquerably fierce.

We can't know the details of Laotse's personal life, but between the essays, poems, journals, letters, and biographies, Emerson's is literally an open book. How did the "American Taoist," as he came to be called posthumously, live out Laotse's Three Treasures?

On the first treasure, love, Emerson is more earthy (Laotse sets a low bar for earthiness), more analytical, and of course more talkative. Emerson believes youthful romantic love is the first step on the path—the ladder—to universal love. Eros, he says, puts us "in training for a love which knows not sex, nor person, nor partiality..."[4] It ultimately leads to "a benevolence which shall lose all particular regards in its general light."[5] Like Laotse, Emerson sees this state of benevolence—the highest rung on the ladder—as "wholly above...consciousness."[6]

I trace the training for love back further than Emerson does. I believe—as psychologists do today—that the seed is planted, if we're lucky, in infancy and early childhood. That seed is a trustworthy intimate bond with our caregivers. My own life tells me that if it was not planted, that model not present, we can, over the years and decades, handbuild ourselves using the raw material of experience—steadily fostering connections with our fellow humans, nature, and the all-embracing Tao. Meditative practices open a direct door into the Tao, into primordial love. Mine may always be a patched-up bond, but I'm incrementally stitching myself into love's fabric.

I have, at times, been blessed with flashes of universal love. One occurred as I walked down the stairs of a South Korean middle school. It was at the end of two years of arduous English teaching in a draconian educational system set in an alien culture. I didn't carry a stick to class as almost every other teacher did, and most of the girls took advantage of this. But in the moments that I descended those wide institutional stairs, I loved every one of them without qualification—the bright ones, the slow ones, the sweet ones, and the surly American-hating ones. I felt heat; I felt my heart swelling and radiating and engulfing me and the entire building. It was the best of what I could give those dear girls and the best that they gave me.

We can't know how well-nurtured Emerson was as a child and of course nature is as strong a force as nurture, but starting with his earliest journal entries, Emerson berates himself for an innate coldness, an inability to be easy and intimate with people. He was accused by women friends such as the poet Caroline Sturgis and the powerful intellect and feminist Margaret Fuller of what Fuller called "inhospitality of soul."[7] He struggled to correct this defect and responded by reaching out to both women, saying "I shall never go quite back to my old arctic habits."[8] He defends himself to Sturgis, telling her that he had been stung by an earlier disappointment with Anna Barker, another young friend with wit and beauty who married one of his protégés. He writes to Sturgis, "I dare not engage my peace so far as to make you necessary to me, when the first news I may hear is that you have found…your mate, and my beautiful castle is exploded to shivers."[9] Perhaps I should say that these were surely platonic relationships and all three women were friends and companions to Emerson's wife, Lidian, as well. Emerson was a passionate man and his life had the usual human complications.

Emerson acknowledges the fascination we have with romantic love. As he says, "What do we wish to know of any worthy person so much as how he has sped in the history of this sentiment? What books in the circulating library circulate?"[10]

Emerson's first wife—his beloved Ellen, a budding poet—died of tuberculosis only a year and a half after their marriage. He remarried at thirty-two and he and Lidian were together for forty-seven years, until his death. They were certainly well matched in many ways, and yet in his journals, he alternately extols the virtues of marriage and rails against the institution. At forty he complains of "the vitriolic acid of marriage," and nine years later concludes that "everything is free but marriage."[11] These are not the kind of quotations we find on greeting cards, or emblazoned on the walls of libraries, or selected as epigraphs.

Yet around the same time that he's feeling imprisoned by marriage, he and Lidian seem to arrive at a renewed, mutual harmony. He journals, "Love is temporary and ends with marriage. Marriage is the perfection love aimed at, ignorant of what it sought. Marriage is a good known only to the parties. A relation of perfect understanding, aid, contentment, possession of themselves and of the world, —which dwarfs love to green fruit."[12] Of course by love here, he means Eros.

In his poem, "Give All to Love," published when he was forty-four, he advises abandoning oneself utterly to passionate romantic love. But he concludes by cautioning the readers to hang onto their self-reliance in the midst of the turbulence, because the beloved may decide to flit at any time. True to Emerson's optimistic theory of compensation, he counsels that Eros is only a half-god and "when the half-gods go, the gods arrive"—the disappearance of Eros reveals the presence of a much larger divinity. Again, for Emerson romantic love is the entry way to universal love.

Yet it's friendship that seems to be his most reliable source of love. Emerson believes it's these deep connections that make life bearable. "After so many ages of experience," he asks, "what do we know of nature or of ourselves? …In one condemnation of folly stand the whole universe of men. But the sweet sincerity of joy and peace which I draw from this alliance with my brother's soul is the nut itself whereof all nature and all thought is but the husk and shell." This is where he goes on to say that friendship is the solidest thing he knows.[13]

Emerson's writing and life flesh out the everyday, imperfect experience of love, one that we can all relate to. He tells the story of the hard scrabble up the mountain; Laotse addresses us from the summit.

Laotse's choice for the second treasure is likely to come as a surprise to Westerners. Lin Yutang translates it as "never too much." Lin also uses the words "not doing too much" and "restraint," all aimed at building up "reserve power." "Reserve" is a term I use in T'ai Chi to indicate that the joints are never locked; there's always a little bend—to allow qi and blood to flow and to provide a protective cushion against impact. Locked joints stop the flow of blood and internal energy, and in a fight, locked joints get broken. In life, I think it means don't overextend.

What a concept! Our culture is *about* overextending. If we're not overextended, we suspect we're lazy and not doing enough. When we run into each other, the question is always "Keepin'" busy?" The stock answer is yes. I found myself answering yes even when it wasn't true—as if saying no would be a confession of inadequacy or lack of consequence in the world. I was embarrassed to reply any other way.

So some years ago I tried an experiment. When anyone asked me that question, I said no. There was a stunned pause while people tried to figure out how to react. Should they pity me because I'm not functioning properly and possibly ill? Or just feel irritated with me for not having my lines memorized so we can both rush off unthinkingly to the next thing. If I filled in by describing my unhurried life and how I relished it, most faces softened as they caught the feeling of the pace.

I had twinges of guilt when I did this to a person because all of us (I'm no exception) can at times find ourselves squeezed by life's imperatives into a frantically busy state. I believe most people yearn for space to release and expand into. They want more time to think and daydream and putter, more opportunity to live a spontaneous, creative life. Saying no, I'm not busy felt like bragging about having something that wasn't available to them—at least not then.

Sometimes we just *think* it's not available to us. We're going with the ambient flow, not choosing or unchoosing our activities, not permitting our lives to take their own shape at their own pace, emerging as unique works of art. I agree with Marion Woodman, the Canadian Jungian psychologist, who says that life is essentially slow.[14] No wonder I'm drawn to T'ai Chi.

Hemingway said about his writing that he always left some water in the well at the end of the day so it could fill up for tomorrow. When I'm under stress for too long—not enough time for solitude, self-reflection, and daydreaming—my well runs dry. I'm scatter-brained, self-absorbed, irritable, and depressed. I don't sleep well and that compounds the problem. What energy I have mostly goes toward keeping my own head above water; there's little energy or patience for buoying up others.

When I'm depleted, I try hard not to reveal or spread my state to people in the T'ai Chi classes, but the quality of my teaching fluctuates with the level of water in my well. Sometimes exhausted students slump into class looking bleary and distracted. They're unfocused and off balance; it's harder for them to move gracefully and learn new movements; and they have a dispiriting effect on me and the other students. Overextended people are not the only ones affected by their exhaustion. We have a ripple effect that rocks everyone around us; we subtly but very effectively drain energy from our surroundings.

While Laotse says "never too much," well-meaning humanists who are painfully well-informed of the world's cruelty and injustice are likely to say "it's never enough." They're right of course—society's needs are limitless, but an individual is limited. This is where self-love and the ability to set healthy boundaries has to come in.

Keep your mouth shut,
Guard the senses,
And life is ever full.
Open your mouth,
Always be busy,
And life is beyond hope.[15]

I encounter people who I "see" and sense as spinning spheres. I can be one myself. Like a good martial artist deflecting opponents, we're whirling, repelling anyone who approaches too close, anyone who might need something from us. We can't take in one more thing; there's no reserve power; we're not available. It's the opposite of the face we want to present to the community. While busily working to set the world right, we're undermining our own efforts, contributing to the imbalance. Fortunately the radiating ripple effect also works in reverse—relaxed, well-rested people leading a balanced life draw us in, soothe, and nourish us. They're in short supply.

We're all made differently. I'm someone who's easily overbooked and needs to retreat into unscheduled time to replenish myself. I may start by sitting and staring off into space, letting my mind run off leash—one of my favorite pastimes. Eventually I'll seep like water into whatever mental or physical channel spontaneously opens up. There's no "ought to." Inspiration comes unbidden and unexpected from this quiet, amorphous place—or it doesn't. Either is okay. This place has no purpose, no goal. Not everyone requires as much low-vibrational time as I do, but it's good if we know our needs and *respect* them.

When I was about eleven, my father, an M.D., told me about an experiment done by Hans Selye, a Canadian medical researcher who pioneered the concept of the effect of stress on human health. In this experiment, rats were placed in a refrigerated room where the temperature was near freezing. The rats that survived the first two days actually thrived for several months—their coats were shiny and they were very industrious. But at the end of that time, exhaustion set in and all of them succumbed. I recently looked up Selye's record of this experiment in his book *The Stress of Life*. The protocol was more intricate and the conclusions more complex than what I've related, but the point my father made to me—the overarching message—is the same. We can adapt to and even thrive under extraordinarily demanding conditions for a period of time, but eventually our ability to adapt is exhausted. This is when something breaks irrevocably.

All illness on every level of our being—physical, mental, and spiritual—is exacerbated by the stress of overextending. Plenty of illness is *caused* by it. Initially our bodies protest with minor illnesses that run their course and disappear. Eventually, if the stress is unremitting, a chronic or terminal disease manifests. That's how I became type-1 diabetic at the age of fifty. Often misnamed in this country as "juvenile onset diabetes," my inherited gene didn't get triggered until unusually late in life. We understand this sort of thing better now as epigenetics.

Our happiness matters. Our well-being has value. Each one of us—equally and simultaneously—is the center of the universe. Primordial love includes us too. Under extreme circumstances, we may believe we have no choice but to willingly sacrifice ourselves for something we think is more important than we are. But we have to be careful that it's not a simple, neurotic lack of self-love that makes it *easier* for us to martyr ourselves than take care of ourselves. It's essential to recognize that if we reserve and conserve our time and energy, we will have an abundance to give. And where and when to apply that abundance in this overheated culture is a matter for thoughtful, even *disciplined* consideration. Not overextending is a spiritual practice in itself.

One of my students, Rebecca Hamaki, has studied the Chinese language. She told me that the character representing the word "busy" is composed of two radicals. The left-hand radical means "heart," and the right-hand radical means "to die" or "to lose." So the Chinese definition of "busy" is heart is lost or heart dies. This explains why not overextending ranks up there with love in Laotse's three treasures. We can't love with a dead heart.

It's too bad an English version of the *Tao Te Ching* wasn't available to Emerson. He could have used Laotse's advice on not overextending. But it's arguable he had no choice but to be driven.

Waldo's father, the Unitarian minister William Emerson, died when his son was eight. As teenagers, he and his brothers rushed to get themselves educated so they could support their mother and each other. After graduating from Harvard at seventeen, he joined his older brother William in the first of several schools for both boys and girls that he and his brothers would open. The teaching was never anything but drudgery to them and a stopgap way to earn money.

Waldo entered Harvard's Divinity school at twenty-two, but was forced to drop out after a few months because of a temporary blindness—probably due to a rheumatic inflammation brought on by a combination of financial stress and too much reading. By writing a sermon that was acceptable to an association of ministers, he earned his license to preach at twenty-three. Though unordained, he began his paid work in the church. Two years later, he re-entered the Divinity School and was ordained in 1829.

This career choice was not made for religious reasons. It gave him a way to support himself and family members while providing an opening toward following his bliss—exercising what he referred to as his "moral imagination" and writing vividly and movingly. From the beginning, the church and its dogma were too confining. Despite the fact that he was very popular with his Unitarian congregation in Boston and surprisingly well paid for his age, his unorthodox ideas brought about the necessary split. When he was twenty-nine, he took the precarious leap into fulltime writing and lecturing. His first wife had died and he would not remarry for three years, but he had his mother and, partially, his brothers to support.

Very quickly, as Emerson's reputation as a speaker and essayist blossomed, his lecturing engagements and touring schedule became relentless, exhausting work. Traveling mostly in fall and winter, first to other New England towns, then to New York and Philadelphia, he gradually extended his range to the Midwest and—as soon as the railroad tracks were completed—all the way to California.

For a long time he organized his own venues and advertising. His accommodations were mostly uncomfortable. In Michigan, he got from one town to another in an open sleigh. His audiences responded with everything from incomprehension to tepid interest to zealous enthusiasm. He succeeded partly because lectures were Americans' primary source of entertainment and because by the time he was fifty, he'd been lionized. Of course he also had something substantive and controversial to say and an understated yet powerful way of speaking. His inner light shone through.

Emerson thought of himself as constitutionally fragile, but considering the demands he made on himself, he held up well—probably because he counter-balanced all the overextending by living in the quiet haven of Concord. There he played with his children, gardened, added to his extensive orchard, and spent time with friends. This home life warmed and softened him. He instinctively made sure he had ways of refilling the well.

Laotse's third treasure is another piece of advice that runs counter to our prevailing culture: Don't try to be first. It means stop the knee-jerk competition, the incessant comparing myself with others. This unhealthy approach to life is generated out of fear and insecurity and fuels hostility—not just toward those around me but toward myself as well.

Always trying to be first shuts me off, shrinks me down, makes me rigid and impervious. I wall myself off in a state of tension and apprehension. So I lose out. I can't take in anything new. Backing off and removing myself from the contest, on the other hand, lets me relax, become expansive and *porous*. There are no barriers to my delighting in and absorbing what others have to offer. I become a bigger person. I can *learn*. As Laotse says, "One who never longs to be first in the world is able to achieve the full growth of his capacity." It's ironic that not competing frees us to reach a higher level of achievement.

People who need to be first have to make a psyche-wrenching adjustment in order to make it through a beginning T'ai Chi class. Anyone who studies T'ai Chi knows it's an exercise in humility. (My students want me to have T-shirts made that say "T'ai Chi—it's harder than it looks.") Those who need to always be the best either acquire the flexibility and fortitude they need to see themselves as a lot clumsier and much less masterful than they thought they were or they drop out. There are so many layers to the art—so many demands made on body, mind, and spirit. And you have to seamlessly *integrate* the three. The Chinese say if you don't learn T'ai Chi in five years, take ten. If you don't learn it in ten, take twenty. No hurry. Some people do learn faster than others, but everyone has a steep learning curve. Feeling shame and frustration because you don't grasp a movement instantly or because you think others are catching on faster than you is an interfering distraction, a self-fulfilling prophecy, and a waste of precious energy. As people get familiar with the *pattern* of encountering a new movement that seems impenetrable at first and then gradually comprehending it piece by piece, they relax. Through repeated experience with movement after movement, they come to know that no movement is beyond them and they can learn an entire sequence—in their own time. Meeting the challenge becomes extremely rewarding and reinforcing. The process is also a confidence-building template for an approach to all life's challenges.

Zen Buddhists call this combination of humility and undistracted focus "beginner's mind." "Use it or lose it" applies to beginner's mind. That's why it's important for me and my students to be continually learning new things. For instance, no matter how experienced I am in practicing other T'ai Chi styles, tackling a new one will test my adaptability, patience, and sense of humor. Having a beginner's mind makes it an enlivening, joyful experience and so much easier.

Parenthetically, I want to say something in defense of competition. Always trying to be first is exhausting and counterproductive, but competition is like everything else—taken to extremes it's destructive, and in moderation it can be beneficial. I've noticed that if I have a class composed entirely of first-time beginners, their progress in learning a sequence is slower than it is when there are returning students in the class who have some proficiency. I think the new people see that it's not just the instructor who can do T'ai Chi, and "if that other student can do it, so can I." A little good-natured competition raises the level of everyone's performance.

As a young man, Emerson actually states in his journal that among the people he most respects, "I wish to be first."[16] He wanted to be known for being cogent and eloquent, and longed to be self-confident and successful. Yet his frank ambition did not, as it often does, make him small and mean-spirited or cause him to diminish the competition.

On the contrary, he had an innate receptivity to genius in others. He was always on the lookout for it, energetically and publicly exalting it and promoting it, often with his own money. He immediately recognized Walt Whitman as a true original and the first genuinely American poet, even though Emerson would have dearly loved to have had that title for himself. He helped

Leaves of Grass gain a wide readership despite the scandalous passages. He worked hard over decades to publish the British philosopher Thomas Carlyle in America; raised (and personally contributed) money for Nathaniel Hawthorne; endorsed Bronson Alcott's revolutionary ideas on education, underwriting Alcott's trip to England so he could be present for the opening of a school based on his design; and of course was a friend and financial mainstay to Thoreau. When Thoreau was still at Harvard and in danger of being expelled for rebelliousness, Emerson wrote a letter to the administration to persuade them not to kick him out. Thoreau's hut on Walden Pond was built on Emerson's land and he lived for months at a time with the Emerson family. That's a partial list of the ingenious people supported by an ingenious man. In his wanting to be first, Emerson had room for helping others to be first as well.

Laotse's three treasures evoke an image of a spherical fountain. Love is the central source and the other two treasures spray outward in all directions and loop back into it, endlessly circulating. Embodying universal love, one resides in a state of composed reserve, naturally defending against doing too much because the gentle rain of tz'u falls on oneself as it does on all creation. And when one loves in the biggest sense, there's no impulse to differentiate and compare, no need to restrain the trajectory of others in order to feel better about oneself—we rise and fall and rise and fall together.

His chapter on the three treasures is one of the places where Laotse contradicts the neutrality of the Tao. Rather than saying it's simply a limitless font of neutral energy that doesn't favor any person, thing, or cause, he concludes this chapter by asserting that love is invincible and "Heaven arms with love / Those it would not see destroyed."

These three treasures—love, don't overextend, and don't try to be first—are inseparable spiritual truths. Isn't it interesting that people needed to hear this 2,500 years ago as much as we do now?

CHAPTER NINE NOTES

1. Lin Yutang, transl. and ed., *The Wisdom of Laotse*, (New York: Random House Modern Library, 1948), Ch. 67, p. 291-2.
2. Chang Chung-yuan, transl. and ed., *Tao: A New Way of Thinking*, (New York: Harper & Row Harper Colophon Books, 1975), translator's commentary in Ch. 67, p. 180.
3. Ralph Waldo Emerson, "The Over-Soul," in *Essays, Poems, Addresses* (New York: Walter J. Black Classics Club, 1941), p. 207.
4. Emerson, "Love," in *Essays, Poems, Addresses*, p. 184.
5. Ibid., p. 173.
6. Ibid., p. 184.
7. Emerson, quoted in *Emerson: The Mind on Fire*, by Robert D. Richardson, Jr. (Berkeley, University of California Press, 1995), p. 338.
8. Ibid.
9. Ibid.
10. Emerson, "Love," in *Essays, Poems, Addresses*, p. 175.
11. Emerson, quoted in *Emerson: The Mind on Fire*, p. 331.
12. Emerson, quoted in *Emerson: The Mind on Fire*, p. 470.
13. Emerson, "Friendship," in *Essays, Poems, Addresses*, p. 194.
14. Marion Woodman, *Conscious Femininity*, (Toronto: Inner City Books, 1993)
15. Gia-fu Feng and Jane English, transl., *Tao Te Ching*, (New York: Random House Vintage Books, 1972), Ch. 52.
16. Emerson, quoted in *The Life of Ralph Waldo Emerson*, by Ralph L. Rusk (New York: Columbia University Press, 1949), p. 104.

TEN

UNLEARNING

The student of knowledge (aims at) learning day by day;
The student of Tao (aims at) losing day by day.[1]

Both Laotse and Emerson were bookish men. As an archivist, Laotse was surrounded by the accumulated Taoist writings. As a writer and lecturer, Emerson needed to gain the ear and respect of his audience by demonstrating that he was familiar with the canon, which was vast. He sometimes strikes me as a deliberate name-dropper.

But Emerson knows that intellectual knowledge is both limited and limiting. Books can be "the best of things, well used; abused, among the worst."[2] The lop-sidedness of many scholars disqualifies them from seeing the whole truth—"nature hates calculators."[3] He believes that we can only learn what's worth knowing by living; developing character is more important than developing intellect.[4] Emerson admits he owes many valuable insights to ordinary people who casually toss off ideas that he has been struggling to formulate and put into words for a long time.[5] (Some of the most enlightened people I've known had no academic education above high school. They simply lived sincerely and unpretentiously and bloomed in the course of life. They would have had no use for the word "enlightened.") When we abandon ourselves to our spontaneous "better instincts," Emerson says, we tap into a well of creative genius that far exceeds conscious intellect. Instead of being tyrannized by facts, we can watch those facts fall into place, confirming and supporting inspiration.[6]

Laotse agrees that supreme wisdom precedes and is not dependent on logic and rationality:

> *In the remote past, the man who was good in Tao*
> *   did not lead his people to calculative thinking,*
> *But let them remain ignorant of it.*
> *The difficulty in cultivating men is that they are*
> *   full of intellectual discrimination.*
> *Governing the nation through intellectual*
> *   discriminationis harmful to it.*
> *Not governing the nation through intellectual*
> *   discrimination is a blessing to it.*
> *…It is the reversal of ordinary things, yet it leads*
> *   to great harmony with Tao.*[7]

Laotse and Chuangtse lived in a time of constant war. Confucian and Motsean scholars traveled from state to state, offering their conflicting advice to leaders—advice that Taoists felt added to the pandemonium. Chuangtse is dismayingly prescient when he describes the damage done by too much emphasis on intellectual knowledge:

> *For all men strive to grasp what they do not know, while*
> *none strive to grasp what they already know; …That*
> *is why there is chaos. Thus, above, the splendor of the*
> *heavenly bodies is dimmed; below, the power of land and*
> *water is burned up, while in between the influence of the*
> *four seasons is upset.*[8]

I see Laotse's concept of unlearning operating in my life on several levels—concurrently. There's the daily combining of learning and unlearning—navigating the wordy material world while balancing that with a presence in the wordless Tao.

On a longer timeline, I've traveled round and round between phases of learning and unlearning. I've come out of a cocoon to become a certain person and then gone back into the cocoon to re-form and morph into a new person. I've done this several times. I think of it as going back and forth between the "somebody" stage and the "nobody" stage. The nobody stage—the time of unlearning, leaving the old creature behind and not knowing what new creature will emerge or how long it will take—is part of leading an authentic life. It's a repeating, healthy cycle of growth and decay.

And finally there's the lifelong cycle: In youth and middle age, one diligently takes in knowledge and in the final phase one leaves that knowledge behind, transcending it. As I age, I feel a growing pull toward the blank slate that's cleared for a writing without words. This is the principle of return. We start out without words and we revert to that state.

As I write this, I'm two months from retiring after twenty-eight years of teaching T'ai Chi. I can already feel my practices changing. I'm shedding the rules, the principles that I stress over and over again to my students. A solo practice of T'ai Chi is quite different from a teaching practice. Teaching is a very self-conscious endeavor. Everything must be extremely distinct. I have to think: How do I explain this? What's the best wording? What needs to be said? What doesn't need to be said? What needs to be repeated? My solo practice (always outside) is much more internal and silent. The natural evolution of the Wu style is toward nonmovement—gestures become increasingly muted, yet increasingly powerful. That's the direction I was going in the ten years I practiced before I started teaching. That process was interrupted, and I want to go back to it. I want to experiment, let myself wander away from the heap of conscious knowledge and roam about in the immaterial world. It's a natural progression.

We are so far beyond words. Even I cannot read my own true message. The mystery acts through me, surpassing consciousness, only tantalizingly and fleetingly glimpsed (enough so I'm certain it's there). Like the skywriter, I hope others read something good in that feathery trail. Besides, "The action of the soul is oftener in that which is felt and left unsaid than in that which is said..."[9] And the truth is so simple, Emerson notes, that writers may as well be "bottling a little air in a phial."[10]

In his last years, Emerson did literally unlearn. He suffered from aphasia, the loss of the ability to remember and understand words. It was a gradual process, and he was aware of it. "We remember that we forget," he wrote.[11] He could summon a sense of humor about it, but it was initially very distressing. Gradually, as he entered further into that wordless place, it no longer bothered him. Three years before his death, Emerson's daughter, Edith, wrote to Carlyle, "Mother often says that he is the happiest person she ever knew—he is so uniformly in good spirits, and waking each morning in a joyful mood."[12]

> *Where can I find a man who has forgotten words so*
> *I can have a word with him?*
> —Chuangtse

CHAPTER TEN NOTES

1. Lin Yutang, transl. and ed., *The Wisdom of Laotse*, (New York: Random House Modern Library, 1948), Ch. 48, p. 229.
2. Ralph Waldo Emerson, "The American Scholar," in *The Annotated Emerson*, David Mikics, ed., (Cambridge, MA: The Belknap Press of Harvard University Press, 2012), p. 77.
3. Emerson, "Experience," in *The Annotated Emerson*, p. 238.
4. Emerson, "The American Scholar," in *The Annotated Emerson*, p. 80 and 82.
5. Ralph Waldo Emerson, "The Over-Soul," in *Essays, Poems, Addresses* (New York: Walter J. Black Classics Club, 1941), p. 212.
6. Emerson, "History," in *The Annotated Emerson*, p. 155.
7. Chang Chung-yuan, transl. and ed., *Tao: A New Way of Thinking*, (New York: Harper & Row Harper Colophon Books, 1975), Ch. 65, p. 174.
8. Chuangtse, quoted in Lin Yutang, Ch. 65, p. 287.
9. Emerson, "The Over-Soul," in *Essays, Poems, Addresses*, p. 212.
10. Ibid., p. 220.
11. Emerson, quoted in *Emerson: The Mind on Fire*, by Robert D. Richardson, Jr., (Berkeley: University of California Press, 1995), p. 569.
12. Emerson, quoted in *Emerson: The Mind on Fire*, p. 571.

Margaret Emerson

ELEVEN

BALANCE

There is an inherent balance between Tao and Te because they mirror each other. Light ricochets back and forth between them, illuminating both. The immaterial world, the Tao, is faithfully reflected in Te—the maturity and virtue of the Sage. And not only in the Sage but also in the rest of the Ten Thousand Things, the offspring of the Tao.

> *By knowing the mother*
> *one knows her children*
> *By knowing her children*
> *one comes to know her*
> *Such is their unity*
> *that one does not exist without the other*[1]

If I can observe the seen world with clarity, I can better apprehend the unseen world. I use outsight to gain insight—penetrating further and further into myself, knowing myself more and more deeply, getting closer and closer to my home and anchorage in the Tao.

> *Using the outer light, return to insight,*
> *And in this way be saved from harm.*
> *This is learning constancy.*[2]

I moor myself between two equal and opposite forces—the pull of the material world and the pull of the immaterial world. It's more likely I—and the society I live in—will become unmoored by losing connection to the latter. We center ourselves by not letting go of the Tao.

> *The great Way is easy,*
> *yet people prefer the side paths.*
> *Be aware when things are out of balance.*
> *Stay centered within the Tao.*
>
> *When rich speculators prosper*
> *while farmers lose their land;*
> *when government officials spend money*
> *on weapons instead of cures;*
> *when the upper class is extravagant and irresponsible*
> *while the poor have nowhere to turn—*
> *all this is robbery and chaos.*
> *It is not in keeping with the Tao.*[3]

Wu Wei—effortless effort, poised between action and inaction—is another form of balance. Hang back (don't overextend, don't try to be first). Allow your energy to rise until it naturally overflows into action. Work gets done without forcing it. The way the Way works is to be "free from action, yet nothing is not acted upon."[4] If Sages model this, the people will follow, bringing the community into harmony with itself and with the Tao. This echoes Emerson's belief that the best leaders are influencers, not dominators. The Sage and Laotse's ideal society stay stable by being supple, responsive, and spontaneous—going with the flow. Stability through motion.

Wu Wei can be a very narrow balance beam. If at any time during this exquisitely tuned creative process, conscious *intention* arises—a plan, a concrete goal outside of the moment-to-moment experience—that distracting, distant focus will pull the Sage off beam. Confusion and strife will ensue. She must jump back on, re-inhabit the Tao, return to nondifferentiating, cease making judgments about what the end point should be, and allow human nature—her own and others'—to unfold without interference.

That's not all, however. It gets more complicated:

To experience the original non-differentiation of the nameless, one
should also be free from intending to have no-intention.
To be free from intending to have no-intention is to be quiescent.
Thereby, the world is naturally led to tranquility.[5]

A tall order. How can one get back to no-intention without first noticing the presence of intention and then deliberately abandoning it (intending to have no-intention)? Once intention enters, are we sunk? Yet I know from my T'ai Chi practice and meditation that there is a state that overtakes me *unawares* in the midst of thought and even in the midst of intending to have no thought. Inner stillness relaxes barriers and permits the Tao to enter, lifting me into a transcendent state of pure nondifferentiation, pure oneness.

"Can you enter and leave the realm of Non-being and let those actions take place by themselves? ...This is called the mystic attainment."[6] The Sage straddles Being and Non-being, Wu Wei-ing back and forth over the threshold, unintentionally knitting the two together.

Laotse impresses on me more than once that the Tao is *real* and operating in the world. All existence is inescapably swept up in its net. It's up to me to pay attention, become familiar with its ways, and fashion my life and being in its image. Staying rooted in the Tao, I can make my way toward that tantalizing state of unwavering equanimity in which I'm "happy under prosperous and adverse circumstances alike,"[7] and, at least metaphorically, "beyond death."[8] I have a ways to go.

Emerson roots himself in the Inner Guide—his wormhole to the Over-Soul, the "voice of God" that speaks unfiltered to each of us.[9] "The only right is what is after my own constitution, the only wrong what is against it." Society's wobbling, unreliable labels of good and bad are pierced like tissue paper by the iron compass that directs his path, one new, unplanned step at a time.[10] He can sound so sure of himself. But we know—as does he—that he's not immune to being pushed off course by society's rules and circumstances originating outside himself.

Speaking not just for himself but for all of us, Emerson believes the human constitution naturally runs to excess and only a titanic struggle can keep us from being lopsided.

> ...*every good quality is noxious, if unmixed, and, to carry the danger to the edge of ruin, nature causes each man's peculiarity to superabound. ...A man is a golden impossibility. The line he must walk is a hair's breadth. The wise through excess of wisdom is made a fool.*[11]

It was a lifelong struggle for Emerson to counterbalance the Unitarian rationalism that had been drummed into him from birth. He was painfully aware that his early sermons were cold, abstract, and dull. He had to liberate and cultivate the emotional and intuitive side of himself; become whole, not half; combine body and soul with mind—in his writing and his life.

Overextending constantly threatened to pull Emerson off-kilter. "Ah we busy bodies! ...We talk too much, & act too much, & think too much. ...With the eagerness to grasp on every possible side, we all run to nothing."[12] If we don't allow time for the "vital force" in us to accumulate, we're too depleted to transmute thought into action. We must be mindful of our limitations. While writing this book and trying to absorb and interlace Laotse and Emerson with each other and with my own thoughts, I came across exactly what I needed to hear: "Take what your brain can, and drop all the rest."[13] Fittingly, it appears in the essay "Power."

Despite his fame for advocating self-reliance, Emerson understands the human need—his own need—for its counterpart, community. Self-reliance does not mean self-sufficiency. And only a genuinely strong person can admit that. Early in life, his soul connection with Ellen Taylor brought home his "unbounded dependence."[14]

Emerson's theory of compensation is a theory of balance. It's nuanced and far-reaching He sees polarity in every expression of nature—in night and day, hot and cold, male and female. Everything is half and implies its other half. By definition, poles never occur in isolation; they can't escape one another and are continuously pushing, pulling, and offsetting each other.[15] (Laotse compares the Tao to the bending of a bow—when the width is extended, the length is shortened.)[16]

We cannot dodge this. We can't partake of one end of a thing without being in contact with the other end, as much as we might like to. There's a price to be paid for trying to detach and compartmentalize. Emerson cites the example of sex without love, physical without spiritual. We may think we've succeeded in fragmenting ourselves and others, but whether we're conscious of it or not, we—and they—are always whole.[17]

I'm struck by Emerson's poignant metaphor for the unity of nature and the ultimate inseparability of the poles. We may reach out to divide, but: "The parted water reunites behind our hand."[18] We've been grabbing at nature, tearing off parts of our environment for our own ends as if the other parts aren't connected, affected, and being pulled and torn as well. We've finally pulled the pieces

we've been ignoring right up to our face and their woundedness
is threatening our existence. If we can't restore our own balance,
getting rid of us would be nature's way of restoring *her* balance.
"The parted water reunites behind the hand."

Nature is the great equalizer and moderator. "Nothing can
be given, all things are sold."[19] The farmer envies the President
in the White House. But acquiring so conspicuous an office
"has commonly cost him all his peace and the best of his man-
ly attributes." He must be "content to eat dust behind the real
masters who stand erect behind the throne."[20] Genius likewise
has its drawbacks. Because she never stops innovating, her new
ideas will supplant her old ones, and she'll be called a traitor, a
betrayer by followers who can't keep up.[21]

I find myself reading Emerson's essay "Compensation" wanting
him to tell me that I've been seeing things wrong. What I see is
rampant unfairness in human relations—credit not being given
where credit is due, good deeds punished as often as rewarded,
and evil-doers getting off scot-free. I want to hear that the scales
level out inexorably and promptly, meaning the good are vindicated
and the bad get their comeuppance *in my lifetime*. And at times he
delivers. He rejects the Christian preaching that we have to wait
until after we die for justice to be meted out—in heaven or hell.

"Things refuse to be mismanaged for long," Emerson assures
me. "Though no checks to a new evil appear, the checks exist
and will appear."[22] Sounds good. And this sounds even better:

> *Justice is not postponed. ...Every secret is told, every crime
> is punished, every virtue rewarded, every wrong redressed,
> in silence and certainty. What we call retribution is the
> universal necessity by which the whole appears wherever
> a part appears. If you see smoke, there must be fire. If you
> see a hand or a limb, you know that the trunk to which
> it belongs is there behind.*"[23]

Then he hedges, saying reckoning may be spread over a long time and may not come clear to us for many years.[24] Eventually our intermittent moments of individual and communal "sanity" will reveal to us the settling of accounts and justify the martyrs.[25] Isn't that a little late for the martyrs?

Also, retribution may be more internal than external, more spiritual than physical, more invisible than visible. "Treat men as pawns and ninepins, and you shall suffer as well as they. If you leave out their heart, you shall lose your own. ... All infractions of love and equity in our social relations are speedily punished. They are punished by fear."[26] In other words, tyrants cannot encounter their victims without sensing their hatred and hostility and feeling threatened, vulnerable, and paranoid. I can grant that, though in some cases the fear may be subliminal. A more concrete punishment would be more satisfying. Dorian Grey can stay so infuriatingly unblemished and robust to our eyes. I have observed, however, that—just as Laotse points out—greedy, acquisitive people are plagued by an ever-present fear of losing what they have.

Envy is one of the dominant driving forces in humans. "How can Less not feel the pain; how not feel indignation or malevolence towards More?" But it is in the nature of the soul—the collective, unified human soul—to compensate for these inequalities. "Yours" and "mine" melt away and we are all enriched by each other's accomplishments and good fortune.[27] I wonder if anyone ascends to a level where the knee-jerk twinges of envy are wholly eliminated. If Emerson felt them, he not only did not act on them, he transmuted them into a celebration of other people.

We are compensated for personal tragedy by inner growth. Although devoured by a black hole without any discernible pinpoint of light, we emerge—after the passage of time—on the other side, changed, and living life on a new spiritual level.[28] "...whatever lames or paralyzes you, draws in with it the divinity, in some form, to repay."[29] I know that to a recent victim of ca-lamity this can sound glib and insensitive, but Emerson speaks from hard experience, having lost his first wife and first child.

Some things, Emerson believes, transcend the workings of his theory of compensation. There is never too much love or wisdom or beauty "when these attributes are considered in the purest sense." There is no "tax" on virtue "for that is the incom-ing of God himself, or absolute existence..."[30] Echoing Laotse, Emerson claims good people are invulnerable to harm. Like fire, they consume and transform everything to their own nature and "disasters of all kinds...prove benefactors."[31]

A concept expressed in "The Over-Soul" that I find very sat-isfying because it agrees with my own experience (including this writing) is that "The things that are really for thee gravitate to thee. ...Every proverb, every book, every byword that belongs to thee for aid or comfort, shall surely come home through open or winding passages."[32] As if my halfness attracts its other half. I've watched this occur throughout my life. Those material and nonmaterial resources I've most needed to support me as I've wholeheartedly pursued my passions have appeared, and have had the quality of, at the very least, delightful coincidences and sometimes full-blown miracles.

In the end, balance can only come from wholeness. "The reason why the world lacks unity, and lies broken and in heaps," Emerson states, "is because man is disunited with himself."[33] I'm indebted to my friend Beverly Allen for the word "re-member." We have to re-member ourselves, retrieve and reassemble the parts we've forgotten or abandoned or severed along the way, over the years and decades; not rejecting or denying any parts of ourselves and our experience—murky, chaotic, and painful as some of it is. Out of this hodgepodge we have steadily been distilling and molding our beings—the lotus growing out of the mud. While I was asleep, an image of the small black purse that I currently carry with me appeared. The image was accompanied by the words "Your baggage is your wealth." All those trunks and suitcases and laundry bags I've filled and lugged around, condensed into one small bag. The gleaning process is ongoing. I keep re-membering pieces of myself, and pulling the nuggets I extract from them into my sphere. I slowly come closer to being rounded and whole.

———◆———

The Taoist symbol of balance is beautiful and strong. If we spend time with it, it teaches us about the constant dance between polarity and unity. We call it yin-yang; the Chinese call it *t'ai chi*:

I need to explain: When I say "I do T'ai Chi," I'm mispronouncing the phrase and lopping off a third of it. My original teacher, Kao Ching-hua, never allowed me to say "I do T'ai Chi." I always had to say "I do T'ai Chi Ch'uan." Saying I do T'ai Chi was like saying I play basket instead of I play basketball. The last word, Ch'uan, literally means "fist," and was used to signify "martial art." (Gradually as more sports were introduced to China, it came to refer to any type of sport or physical exercise.) T'ai Chi Ch'uan is the Taoist internal martial art based on the philosophy of t'ai chi. When I started teaching, I adhered to Kao Ching-hua's rule; but quickly discovered that I was confusing people by using the full name in my advertising, so I caved in and went with the colloquial.

The mispronunciation comes from pronouncing the second word, Chi, with an aspirated sound as in "chair." It really should sound more like a "j." When the Chinese developed their own way of Romanizing their language, they chose to make it all one word: taijiquan. The ch of chi has become a more phonetic j. And the q of the third syllable, quan, is pronounced as an aspirated ch.

Pronouncing "Chi" in T'ai Chi Ch'uan with an aspirated sound has led to the confusion of this word with the word for energy or life force:

Spelled "ch'i" in the British Wade-Giles system of Romanization (the apostrophe indicates an aspirated sound), it's spelled "qi" in the Chinese Pinyin system. I mix the two systems in my writing, using Wade-Giles for T'ai Chi Ch'uan and Pinyin for qi (energy)—I go with whatever I think will be most commonly understood. Regardless of how the words are Romanized, two distinct characters represent them and if pronounced properly, they sound different.

I continue to mispronounce T'ai Chi and I continue to incorrectly use the phrase to refer to both the symbol and the practice based on the symbol.

Probably about 2,000 years old, the t'ai chi symbol may have originally represented the waxing and waning of the moon. As a portrait of equal and opposite forces complementing, supporting, and vying with each other within a process of continuous revolution, it became the recognized emblem of Taoism.

Taoist philosophers say that before t'ai chi there is wu chi— the boundless void. This is Laotse's Tao, which I perceive as a pregnant, neutral energy; nothingness with unlimited potential. Wu chi (stillness) begets t'ai chi (movement): two forces form and pull apart, differentiating themselves. From t'ai chi come the Ten Thousand Things. T'ai chi is the living armature on which the material world is sculpted.

Kao Ching-hua sat me down one evening to demonstrate how to draw the characters for T'ai Chi Ch'uan and explain their derivation. It's the first two that are relevant to us now. This is t'ai:

It represents a person—two strokes overlaying each other at the top to form the torso, and diverging to represent the legs. This person has broad shoulders—a horizontal line just beneath the top. The broad shoulders show that she can handle a lot of responsibility, she's exceedingly mature. The stroke close to the bottom and on the inside of the leg on the left amplifies the meaning—like saying very. By itself, Kao Ching-hua told me, this character means 'the universe." It's a commonly used character, and also just means "big." I like the idea of a pictograph of a person—big in the internal sense of the word—as a microcosm of the universe. We do indeed contain and reflect the universe.

This is chi:

The radical occupies the left half and is a pictograph of a tree. I think of it as depicting the ground, the roots beneath the ground, and the tree above. The right half of the character is a guide to pronunciation. This character means wood or strong—wood is a strong, durable substance.

Put together, Sifu Kao said, the phrase t'ai chi means "the universe and beyond," or "all-encompassing." Common English translations include "supreme ultimate" and "grand terminus." I like the latter because it refers to a wheel, and the first thing you notice about this symbol is that it's round.

The circle denotes wholeness, completeness. The second thing you notice is that it's divided into two halves. And it's not divided with a straight line. A straight line would suggest an inert state. The "s" curve indicates movement, revolution. A more radical "s" curve would make it appear to speed up; a lazier "s" curve would make it slow down.

Then you notice the little dots. They remind us that in the most extreme state of any condition, the seed of its opposite is contained. The black dot is placed in the center of the white at its most full-blown, and vice versa. The t'ai chi symbol often appears without these dots, but even without them you can see the slim beginning of the black where the white is fattest, and the slim beginning of the white where the black is fattest. Yin and yang give rise to each other.

The orientation of the symbol as pictured above is the way Kao Ching-hua's tradition required it to be drawn and displayed. The symbol appears all over the world in myriad variations—the "s" curve could be reversed; the symbol could be turned on its side or upside down; the dots could be omitted.

In this positioning, the top is north, the bottom south, the right east, and the left west. The white side is the sun rising in the east. The qualities of day, heaven, heat, vigorous activity, and male are associated with this, the yang side. On the black side—the yin side—is the setting sun, the earth, the moon, night, coolness, stillness, gestation, and female.

This symbol is often thought of as a portrait of harmony. But we may need to expand our associations with that word to allow for the real tug and pull between the two opposing forces, and the continuous change that this tension generates. It's always possible that one force will take over more than half the territory.

The encroached force will have to push back to restore balance. And balance, of course, is the core meaning of the t'ai chi symbol.

We see this dynamic operating in our lives every day. Things go so far one way and eventually they go too far and have to be brought back. Something starts out as a good thing, then grows too big and morphs into a bad thing. (Gas-driven cars seemed like a good idea at one time.) If we're alert, we'll correct before circumstances enter a truly extreme—and thus destructive—state. It is the *extremity* that makes it destructive.

Sometimes it's a matter of *allowing* circumstances to return to their natural state of balance, backing off, getting out of the way, instead of interfering and trying to force an outcome that—it becomes clear—isn't meant to happen. When the boulder I've been pushing up the mountain comes to a standstill for long enough, my feet skidding impotently on the gravel, I reach the point of giving up. When I let go, the boulder rolls back, following the Wu Wei path of least resistance to its rightful angle of repose. "I give up" is a mantra that I've found very useful. It leads to a fresh, more authentic way—an opportunity for rebirth. You *have to give up first*, then the dammed-up energy will cut its own new channel.

One of the first things I learned when I started practicing T'ai Chi is that balance is not a static state. If I stand on one foot, from a distance it may look like I'm perfectly still. But if you get close you can see all the bones, muscles, tendons, and toes working constantly to keep me upright. It would be nice if we could reach a place in our lives where everything is in a comfortable balance and simply stay there. But things around us will inevitably change and we'll change internally as well as externally. What was comfortable, healthy, and positive becomes uncomfortable, unhealthy, and negative—if we don't respond soon enough. So we have to adjust; we have to come to a new balance over and over again.

It's important to note that yin and yang are relative terms. Laotse points out in his second chapter that we only know short in relation to long and back in relation to front. Although T'ai Chi combines yin and yang evenly in each movement and in the sequence as a whole, relative to our culture it's a yin force. It's slow, quiet, and single-focused compared to the frenetic, noisy, multitasking scene we inhabit. Within the world of T'ai Chi there are many different styles, each with its own personality. Relative to the muted, intensely internal Wu style, the Chen style is yang—it mixes slow movements with fast whip-like movements, explosive releases of *fa jin* or force. We think of water as yin when we contrast it with fire. But if you heat water enough, it becomes steam—a yang form of water. And if you cool it down enough, it becomes ice—an extreme yin form of water. When I'm teaching, I'm yang and the students are yin. We leave the studio and our roles may reverse. I may take on a follower (yin) role in relation to some other person or project, and my students may take on leadership (yang) roles.

The practice of T'ai Chi gives me stillness and clarity that help me discern what's the appropriate role to play in a given situation—so I can further the purpose at hand instead of being a hindrance. If I try to usurp the leadership role when that's properly someone else's, I'll just get in the way and be resented for it. An equally effective way to obstruct an enterprise is to hang back in the follower role when it's proper and necessary for me to lead.

Every T'ai Chi movement is an illustration of the interdependence of yin and yang. I can't strike and strike and strike again. Every strike is preceded and followed by pulling back, retreating, gathering. We tend to notice the aggressive, in-your-face part of the movement more than we notice the preparatory part, but not only are they equally important, *they generate each other.*

Here's something I learned from the practice of Silk Reeling about the smooth transfer of weight from one leg to the other.

(Silk Reeling is a foundation-building exercise for T'ai Chi.) Once I've poured one hundred percent of my weight into a leg and I've relaxed the empty leg (the one that just finished pushing the weight to the other side), not only will the weight flow without obstruction back into that leg, there's actually a suctional force *pulling* the weight back. Nature abhors a vacuum. It wants to even things out.

People are one of those things that naturally want to even out. It's not easy to change a person's character, but over time, consistent T'ai Chi practice can penetrate that deep. I physically "go through the motions" of alternating between yin and yang (advancing and then retreating, gathering and then delivering energy) and noticing what I'm doing. Gradually I get pretty good at both. I probably started out much better at one than the other. The newly balanced outer skill is matched by a growing inner skill, whether I expect this to happen or not. My sister says her practice has helped her be more assertive when it's called for. Mine has also helped me to be more assertive when appropriate, as well as more restrained when appropriate. It's a work in progress, but T'ai Chi is reshaping me.

Laotse has lots of practical advice for T'ai Chi practitioners: Avoid extremes, don't overextend—reaching too far makes us lean and pulls us away from our base.[34] This puts us into what martial artists call a "position of disadvantage." A slight tug from our opponent and we're on the ground. Laotse warns us not to stand on tiptoe[35]—holding ourselves too high defies a basic law of physics: the lower our center of gravity, the more stable we are. Self-consciousness is another thing that can wreck our balance. "Putting on a display," boasting, and feeling self-righteous are "'unnecessary luggage.'"[36] It's always when I'm congratulating myself for having done a movement particularly well that I botch the one I'm currently doing.

We all know this law of physics: Every action is matched by an equal and opposite reaction. But in the last years of my practice I've come to a heightened perception of this principle operating in my body—both on the mechanical level and on the energetic level (the movement of qi in and around me). Every force moving up is accompanied by a force moving down at the same time; every force that moves forward moves back; every force that goes left goes right. The forces are connected and elastic, stretching away from each other and pulling themselves back together. I can feel the palm that's moving up in the palm that's moving down. When I do leg lifts (slow-motion kicks), I'm keenly aware of the force rooting into the ground through my supporting leg. That force has to be at least as great as the force emanating from the kicking leg or I'll fall onto it. The supporting leg is like the trunk of a tree; the kicking leg is a branch. Laotse puts it this way: "The heavy is the root of the light. / The unmoved is the source of all movement."[37]

One summer I was standing on green grass in the middle of a soccer field. I lifted my arms and opened my palms to take in energy from the wide-open sky, then lowered my arms slowly to conduct that blue river through my body and into the ground. Unmistakably and simultaneously I felt an equally vital river moving in the opposite direction. They traveled the same bed but neither interfered with the other. The current moving down generated the current moving up; one couldn't exist without the other. It was their partnership that held me vertical and steady.

Here's the important thing: Becoming conscious of this—of something that's normally happening subconsciously—strengthens and magnifies it. Conscious and subconscious working together are much more powerful than either working alone. Each time I'm able to unify those two halves of myself, I get a taste of the wholeness and balance of existence.

There are some T'ai Chi practices when my movement slows so much that I wonder if it will stop altogether. Every particle of my being is fully charged. A feeling of suspension and, at the same time, incredible speed overtake me. I've come up with two possible ways of putting this into words—and they seem to be exact opposites. One is that I feel as if I'm being suctioned out of my familiar space and time and flung into something else, my particles dispersed into a borderless existence that doesn't know space or time. Another is that a gate opens and a fantastic raw energy gushes into my small dot of a being and obliterates me. Either way I vanish into total yang (outward exploding) and total yin (inward imploding) all at once.

The "door" to this state may open and close repeatedly during the sequence. I feel rubbery moving in and out of it. It's an experience beyond words. Not just beyond words, beyond thought. It is possible to stop thinking. I lose my "self." There is no longer subject and object, me and not-me, movement and stillness. The thrilling feeling comes afterward when I return and realize I've been away. I watch for and welcome this phenomenon. It always comes uninvited and unannounced.

Of course this experience—the astonishing merging of yin and yang—radically alters how I perceive the concerns of day-to-day life. It's consoling and calming to know that I and my niggling struggles and even the world and its planet-threatening challenges are a piece of something bigger on an entirely different scale. Laotse says the Tao's inexhaustible energy is impartial and doesn't care if I succeed or not. But I have "seen" it and have a way into it, and can draw on it to sustain me in my material existence. It does not withhold itself.

My almost forty-year-long practice of T'ai Chi and meditation doesn't mean I never get knocked off balance, but it helps me regain my balance more quickly. It also seems to be supplying me with a growing underlying solidarity that's even there when I'm feeling extremely anxious, vulnerable, and shaky. It's outside my consciousness, but I witness its effect in my life.

I try to live every day with one foot in the Tao. I am, on one level, a physical body operating in a material world full of necessary and unnecessary distractions. If I allowed them to, they would consume me. In addition to being unbalanced, that life would be shallow and unfulfilling. But I do not revere the material world any less than I do the immaterial world. My human life on Earth is the precious medium I work with to realize the Tao. Achieving balance between these two worlds is my aspiration and my definition of enlightenment.

My emotions are valuable messengers from the Tao. I try not to let any of them hide under my radar, including the painful, mean-spirited ones—the ones I wish I didn't have. I dive down, grab whatever's there, hold it up to the morning light, turn and examine it from all angles. I can't decide what emotions I have, but once I know an emotion, I can try to figure out where it came from and decide whether and how to act on it. Unknown, buried emotions fester, poisoning my actions until they're exhumed. People classify some emotions like anger and envy as "negative" and part of their "shadow side." And they're afraid of their shadows. If we're courageous enough to look, our shadow side becomes our light side, illuminating the truth of our being. (A happy side effect of this process is that it keeps us humble.)

I frequently hear the phrase "What is is," meaning we must accept what befalls us. It's true that acceptance makes life much easier—no sense fighting against past or current circumstances we have no power to change. It's futile and a waste of energy. But we can't skip the initial trauma and the natural, human, healing stages that bring us gradually to genuine acceptance. I have seen "What is is" used by people to admonish themselves to shove aside instinctive emotions triggered by disappointment or tragedy. It's as if people want to avoid the anguish of slogging through those feelings or they think they should be too enlightened, too detached by now to still be prey to something so primitive and messy. The contradiction is that emotions are part of what is. Human suffering is here to stay. Through my body I encounter the laws of nature and I *learn*. The more thoroughly I accept and unify with my own nature, the more I unify with the nature of all existence.

It took the help of a psychotherapist and a technique called EMDR for me to fully embrace and make peace with emotions that had been undermining my psychic balance since childhood. I wish I'd experienced EMDR (eye movement desensitization and reprocessing) decades before I did. I was sixty-four when a therapist friend suggested I try this method for dealing with childhood trauma. It's commonly used for vets suffering from PTSD.

Typical of more recent developments in EMDR, my therapist and I did not use eye movement. Instead, I sat comfortably in a chair, upraised palms resting on either leg. With eyes closed, I silently recalled a traumatic incident that occurred when I was around eight years old—one I'd previously described to my therapist. Sometimes she would ask questions and I would answer (relating thoughts, associations, and physical sensations), and sometimes we were silent. During the silent times, the therapist tapped her finger alternately on my right and left palms. Through repeated visits over some months, I stood in the presence of my more than fifty-year-old pain, outrage, sadness, and confusion. But this time as a strong, compassionate adult. The nurturing and soothing I didn't receive at the time I could give to myself now. The incident gradually lost its charge and the insecurity, anxiety, and depression it triggered faded. The tapping stimulated both sides of my brain and nervous system. To my grateful surprise, this *rebalancing* triggered a foundational shift deep within me that has put me—permanently—on a stronger emotional footing.

The culture that raised me is underdeveloped when it comes to exploring and trusting human emotions and intuition. Its intellectual talents superabound and run to excess. Intellect likes to simplify things by dismembering them, then looking at one piece at a time and conveniently forgetting it's not the whole thing. I've known intellectuals who reject thinking that's "contaminated" by intuition. It's because intuition is personal, subjective, sometimes illogical, sometimes irrational, and—worse—opens the door to emotions and the physical sensations that come with them. Intuition complicates things. (Intellect can complicate things for people who only like to use their intuition.) It's so much easier to discount thinking and writing that include intuitive experience. This is a fear reaction by people who haven't explored this side of themselves, don't understand it, and are afraid to try. Subliminally they know they're missing something—refusing to take in the whole picture—and this makes their reaction all the more vehement. The prevalence of this bias is an indication of how saturated we are with the imbalance of a patriarchal society. The rational masculine principle is elevated and the intuitive feminine principle is suppressed.

Translating the *Tao Te Ching* requires both intellect and intuition. The scholarship has to be there (although no scholar can be entirely sure of the meaning of the ancient Chinese characters). And intuition is required to grasp the full intent because Laotse is a man of few words who writes intuitively and poetically. There are no detailed explanations or signposts telling us which way to go with stanzas and chapters, each one of which shines in innumerable directions, spraying mind-boggling rays of thought. We're invited to follow all of them at our leisure.

Of the translations I've read, I think Lin Yutang (a scholar, inventor, and novelist) most consistently "gets" Laotse. Others accomplish this to a greater or lesser degree. As I read a series of translations of the same chapter, I'm using both intellect and intuition. In the end, however, it's intuition that tells me which translation is most true to what Laotse wants to say.

There's evidence that my culture is evolving and coming to see humans in a more balanced, holistic way. Neuroscientists now recognize three "brains" in the body, three places where there is an extraordinarily dense gathering of neurons—in the head, around the heart, and in the abdomen. (All three are connected by the vagus nerve, the longest nerve of the autonomic nervous system, running from the brain stem to the intestines.)

For millennia, Taoists have been aware of the same three crucially important energy centers, which they call *dan tians*. When Taoists refer to *the* dan tian, they mean the one in the abdomen. This is the body's main qi reservoir and qi pump. "Dan" means red and "tian" means field or area. Kao Ching-hua told me it's called "field of red" because at any given time, about twenty-five percent of the blood in the body is accumulated there.

This abdominal dan tian can actually be experienced as both an area and a point. As an area, it comprises the waist, hips, abdomen, lower back, perineum, and our center of gravity. The waist is the biggest, strongest joint in the body. The lower back is the site of the *ming men* or "gate of life"; flattening the lower back opens this gate, allowing qi to flow unobstructed along the energy channels of the head and torso. The perineum is the site of the *hui yin* where many of the yin channels of qi converge. When we stand evenly weighted on both legs, our center of gravity—our physical balance point—is in the middle of the abdomen. So the dan tian is a nexus of vital energy centers.

As a point, it is the hub of all this life. Some say the way to locate this point is to measure two finger breadths below the navel and two finger breadths in; others say it's three finger breadths below the navel and three finger breadths in. I think the best way to find it is intuitively—it's the point of origin of the breath as I expand my abdomen in all directions while inhaling, and contract while exhaling. It's the turn-around point of the breath cycle. The lungs expand too, of course, but the breath begins and ends with the dan tian.

This point occupies no space and yet it is the door to unlimited space. It's my umbilical cord to the universe, through which I have access to everything. Energy courses into the dan tian from the earth and sky and is then pumped out to the furthest reaches of my body, augmented and directed by breath and intention. The immediate sphere of influence of this point is a charged field—the dan tian as an area.

I use the dan tian as both a point and an area, not just while doing T'ai Chi or meditating, but throughout my day. I draw on it in encounters with people and while kayaking, swimming, hiking, writing, and painting. But even as a kid I was aware that my impulses and reactions originated not in my head but in my belly and traveled upward to my heart where I felt them and to my brain where I put them into thoughts and words. I have always regarded what I eventually came to know as the dan tian as the source of my intuition or "gut feelings," the home of my subconscious, and the well from which my dreams spring. When I practice T'ai Chi in the mornings, my intensified connection with the dan tian brings back last night's dreams—dreams I wasn't able to recall with conscious effort on waking.

I experience this lower dan tian as the conductor of the orchestra. It gathers all my resources—physical, mental, and spiritual—and pulls in qi and resources from outside myself to bring me into heightened wholeness and acuity.

I first proved this to myself in 1984 while skiing Mt. Bachelor. I had no business being at the top of that mountain. Wind had whipped the snow into Dairy Queen swirls that—up there— looked sinister. The way down was shockingly steep; there were no trees to hang onto; and I was a mediocre skier. I had only one hope—plug into the dan tian and trust it to give me the wherewithal to make it to the bottom in one piece. Five years of T'ai Chi training had at least begun to teach me what the dan tian was capable of. So instead of giving my attention to the parts of me that appear to do the skiing—my arms and legs—I focused inward on the dan tian. Outside of practicing T'ai Chi or meditating, this was the first time I deliberately drew on that place in the center of my abdomen. I stayed in my dan tian the whole way down the mountain. My limbs performed with strength and coordination far beyond my normal skill. I made it without falling.

The Taoist concept of dan tian has a kindred spirit in the Japanese concept of hara, which translates literally as "belly." A person with hara has the capacity to open herself to the seminal life force and manifest it with increasing faithfulness over a lifetime. The hara resides at the center of gravity.

As I get quiet during sitting or T'ai Chi, there's a natural sinking and settling into the abdomen, into the dan tian. I feel like I'm coming home. Emotions that I've been holding in that area (suppressing or repressing, stuffing them down in order to avoid) have to leave. They're displaced—my essential self is there now. As the prickly emotions drift upward, they pierce heart and head. Conscious and subconscious mingle. I get to know myself better. The process may bring tears or smiles. It's often an unpleasant stage, but it doesn't last. It all keeps going, vaporizing through the crown of my head.

So residing in the dan tian triggers a clearing out. I become empty, occupying a place that I call "nowhere"—I think of it as "going nowhere." Yet at the moment of arrival, I erupt into everywhere. When I practice T'ai Chi overlooking Crater Lake, I can easily contain within my dan tian all that water, all that blue, the rocks of the caldera, and the trees clinging to its edges. Finally what's in that place is an unassailable clarity and peace.

But the abdominal dan tian is only one of three. I know I'm truly "in" that lower dan tian when I feel a brief ache in the third eye—the uppermost dan tian. Engaging the lower dan tian instantly activates the upper. The two poles acknowledge each other and my body feels the connection. I use Taoist breathing exercises to nourish all three dan tians with universal qi and to circulate energy from my primary reservoir in the abdomen to the heart, and from the abdomen to the third eye. To be healthy and whole, I have to be nurturing, aligning, and firing on all three.

I received while meditating that the heart ties together the two poles—head and belly. To oversimplify, the brain in the cranium is intellect, and the brain in the belly is intuition. The head is yang, and the belly is yin. The head is the seat of rational thinking—coming to grips with and navigating the material world. The belly is the Tao itself—exceeding the limits of all possible worldly knowledge, void of distinctions or judgments, filled with primordial love. The heart marries the head with the belly, marries primordial love to action, and the result is courage. Rooted in the Latin word for heart, courage is the mental and moral strength to persevere in the face of danger and fear—to be inspired to orient one's actions consistently day after day toward enhancing life and building love. The heart is the spiritual center of gravity. It's the middle way.

Now I want to come back to the provocative, unbalanced-sounding idea that the Tao itself is female, something I noted in the first chapter. Laotse uses words like "Mother of All Things," "primal mother," "the feminine," "Female," and "Mystic Female" to characterize the Tao, as well as numerous yin images. (In eight translations, I found only three references to the Tao as male.) How could the Tao be female? How could it be yin? It gives birth to yin and yang; it contains them; but it precedes these distinctions. Why would Taoists have what seemed to me to be a one-sided perception of something that has no sides?

As I mentioned before, my first theory was that the Taoists of Laotse's time were subconsciously trying to compensate for a brutal, insecure civilization that was careening lethally to the yang/male side. It was their way of applying weight to the other pan of the scales in an attempt to even things up and bring their world back into balance.

Then a friend loaned me *The Chalice and the Blade in Chinese Culture.* One glance told me it would be enormously important to me. It's a response by Chinese scholars to Riane Eisler's 1987 book *The Chalice and the Blade* and I knew I had to read her book first.

I was aware from studying art history in college and from reading *When God Was a Woman* by Merlin Stone a few decades ago that humans hadn't always lived in an unrestrained patriarchy as we do now. Eisler describes a Neolithic culture ("the chalice") that lasted from about 10,000 BCE to about 3,500 BCE in Europe. It was what she calls a "partnership" culture—a society in which the sexes are linked instead of ranked, a very equalitarian society with an emphasis on mutual dependence and sharing. These prehistoric cultures harvested wild and domestic crops and kept domesticated animals; they had highly developed arts and crafts and decorated their clothing. They did not make weapons. Nomadic patriarchal tribes ("the blade") gradually invaded and subsumed the chalice cultures. That's where we've been for the last 5,500 years—in what Eisler calls the "dominator" culture in which men dominate women and other men.

Eisler's findings spurred Chinese scholars to research their own Neolithic Age to discover if a partnership culture had existed in China as it had in Europe. Sixteen authors—archeologists, historians, and philosophers—published their findings in 1995, in time for the World Conference on Women in Beijing. Eisler was invited to write the foreword to *The Chalice and the Blade in Chinese Culture.*

China did indeed have an ancient and long-lived goddess-worshipping partnership culture. Not only did it exist in the Neolithic, but it stretched into the first dynasty—the Xia (2070-1600 BCE). And there are, today, *living examples* of the partnership model in Yunnan, the mountainous province in China's southwest corner. The rugged, inaccessible terrain has made it possible for isolated pockets of this culture to survive. The Musuo people worship a supreme goddess and their society is matrilineal, communal, and equalitarian. The seminal feminine/masculine, yin/yang relationship—sex—is purely consensual, free-flowing, and can be either short- or long-term. No individual is dependent on any other individual for economic support or help in raising children. People live in clans and the village really does raise the children. Unlike the patriarchal Chinese society, there is no such thing as mercenary arranged marriage, abandoned children, children born out of wedlock, or unwanted widows.[38]

Mr. Wang Bo, a philosopher at Beijing University, concludes that Taoism has its genesis in these feminine-based societies. He names the core values of the Xia Dynasty: esteem for kindness, honesty, and trustworthiness; a love for simplicity, frugality, and plain living; and an attraction to water and the color black.[39] (Both water and black are yin elements. The Chinese have positive associations with black and to this day wear white to funerals.) These are the same values upheld in the *Tao Te Ching*. Mr. Wang Bo also notes that Laotse interprets the Tao itself as feminine.[40]

Now Laotse's nostalgia for a Golden Age, a "Grand Harmony,"[41] when people led simple, agrarian low-tech lives and were good without knowing they were good suddenly seemed more realistic to me. And even real. Some scholars think Laotse was harking back to a time of unusual peace and prosperity that occurred around 1000 BCE. But I think he was harking back a lot further than that—to the Xia and to the Neolithic. Taoism preserves the idea of a real possibility for us—a civilization in which the female principle, embodied in all genders, takes the lead and the male principle acts *in the service of all* those qualities we associate with females—nurturing, sharing, inclusivity, community building, and humility. In other words, yang, the male principle, acts in the service of yin, the female principle.

Yin images permeate the *Tao Te Ching*. Water is a recurring example: "The best of men is like water"[42] and "There is nothing weaker than water / But none is superior to it in overcoming the hard"[43] are just two of them. Water is a model of Wu Wei, the doctrine of inaction and a yin approach to life. It mates with gravity, harmonizes with it, and wouldn't bother trying to flow uphill. We observe water and learn to get where we want to go with the least possible effort, making nature our ally. We do nothing, yet accomplish everything.

The Tao is compared to rivers inevitably finding their way to the ocean.[44] These rivers carve valleys and ravines and the Tao is sometimes called "The Spirit of the Valley."[45] Sages who emulate the Tao are "Lords of the Ravines."[46] In mountainous regions, valleys provide nurturance—warmth and food and protection from the barren cold of higher elevations. And like Eisler's chalice, the valley is a symbol of the receptive female.

Rulers are advised to take on the female role by leading from behind—tuning into and being guided by the opinions and feelings of the people. The humble role works best in dealing with other governments too. Powerful countries win the loyalty of weaker ones by being gracious and avoiding bullying, aggressive behavior. A humble stance disarms hostility between opponents. And only a solid rooting in the Tao can prevent a strong country from falling into dangerous arrogance.[47]

In a confrontation between countries, Laotse knows that remaining tranquil and compassionate is paramount. A government should not initiate war, should be reserved in the fighting, and when forced to defend itself, must be careful not to demonize its opponent. Demonizing others causes a country to lose its three treasures; it becomes its own enemy.[48] In a peace treaty, the Sage knows better than to expect perfect justice and is willing to overlook some things. She has no need to assign blame. Although she holds her own country to the contract, she is not exacting in holding others to it.[49]

Every chapter of the *Tao Te Ching* advising us how to live urges us to lead with the feminine—lead our own lives and be an influence on others guided by the character of yin, not yang. We cannot be yangless. That side of us has to be well developed, no matter what our gender, so we can have agency within ourselves and in the world. Yet the organizing principle is yin.

The constitution of the Sage is yin on the outside and yang on the inside. Laotse describes her as authentic, unpretentious, self-deprecating, gentle, easy-going, and nonconfrontational; she guards her three treasures—love, don't overextend, and don't try to be first. It takes real fortitude to live out these traits, to forge against the current of a mainstream society that doesn't value them and misperceives them as signs of weakness. The Sage is brave without knowing she is brave because she is only instinctively adhering to her nature. Isn't this the ideal? To be true to oneself even under united opposition. The Sage's hardness supports her softness. She has "belly"; she has hara.

When the world talks about "strong" leaders, they're often talking about weak people who are overcompensating by being belligerent and violent. Laotse says that "Who is calm and quiet becomes the guide of the universe."[50] If the universe will only recognize them.

My surprise at Laotse's describing the Tao as female reminded me of another surprise I ran across in the *I Ching*, the *Book of*

Change. More than 3,000 years old, it predates the *Tao Te Ching*. Its authors perceived an unchanging pattern of change operating in the cosmos and in human affairs. They distilled these infinite permutations into sixty-four hexagrams—six lines stacked one on top of the other. The top three lines and the bottom three lines form distinct trigrams. Each line, each trigram, and each hexagram is a stage in a process and has its own personality and influence. Based on a binary system, a line is either broken (__ __) or solid (_____). Because a broken line can morph into a solid line and vice versa, every part in the hexagram is a moving part.

At crossroads in our lives we can "cast" the *I Ching* using coins or yarrow sticks to determine which path is most in accord with prevailing circumstances and thus which path is most likely to lead to success. We may be advised to advance, retreat, or sit still.

It's Hexagrams Eleven and Twelve that puzzled me. The trigram known as Ch'ien, composed of three solid lines, symbolizes heaven, male, active, and yang:

_____
_____
_____

The trigram known as K'un, composed of three broken lines, symbolizes earth, female, passive, and yin:

____ ____
____ ____
____ ____

You would think that heaven over earth, yang over yin, would be an auspicious hexagram:

————————
————————
————————
——— ———
——— ———
——— ———

After all, when we stand outside, heaven *is* above and earth below. Yet it's just the opposite. The name for this configuration (Hexagram Twelve) is P'i, meaning stagnation and obstruction. Because heaven naturally rises upward and earth naturally sinks downward, they pull apart, polarizing into extremes. There is no mingling, no intercourse, no communication between them; and therefore no harmonizing or balancing of yin and yang. Under these circumstances, mean-spirited people advance while superior people are forced to retreat. Hexagram Twelve is one of the least favorable hexagrams a person can draw.

The preceding hexagram, Eleven, reverses the trigrams, putting earth (yin) on top and heaven (yang) on the bottom:

It's called T'ai, meaning peace. (A homonym with the T'ai in T'ai Chi Ch'uan.) Instead of pulling apart, yin naturally sinks downward into yang and yang naturally rises upward into yin. They mix and pervade each other, creating a balanced blend of yin and yang. This hexagram augurs the advancement of superior people while mean-spirited people are forced to retreat. It's one of the most favorable hexagrams.

I see now that Hexagrams Eleven and Twelve express what Laotse is saying throughout the *Tao Te Ching*: "The big and strong belong underneath / The gentle and weak belong at the top."[51]

At the close of my T'ai Chi classes, we bow and salute each other. In our tradition, the right hand makes a fist and on the left hand, the thumb is tucked in against the palm as a symbol of humility and the fingers are pressed together as a symbol of friendship. The left hand covers the right. Yin over yang. Trained martial artists know you don't approach people fist-first; you approach them with humility and friendship. And as Laotse recommends, you keep your weapons hidden.[52]

Building a society around the masculine principle while suppressing the feminine principle is unsustainable. It results in a progressively less humane and more destructive culture—destructive to all its members and their environment. Right now we're in the position of always trying (mostly unsuccessfully) to put the brakes on a rampaging yang and suffering its ravages. There's no chance for harmony or balance between yin and yang under these conditions. Without a lid, yang erupts, overflows like molten lava, wiping out everything in its path. For the United States, Donald Trump is the natural end-product. He's the perfect case in point to prove Laotse's argument that the proliferation of laws is a sign of the decline of a society: Trump violates conventional norms and restraints, so more laws will have to be devised to keep him and others from doing things people before him didn't need laws to persuade them to do.

Balance works in mysterious ways. On the face of it, it may seem unbalanced to prioritize either yin or yang. But all we need to do is look around us to see that organizing around yang results in ruinous imbalance. Yin has to lead and direct yang. That's how balance—and the preservation of harmonious life—is achieved.

Sometimes I think the human species peaked in the Neolithic Age. It seems so improbable that we could get back to Laotse's Grand Harmony. To start, there are too many of us, and most of us don't live in small villages. Knowledge and science have exploded and we are gluttons for higher and higher technology. We have no restraint, no morals or ethics to guide or rein in our intellectual and material appetites. Like children, we are unable to regulate ourselves. And we're becoming further and further estranged from our own holistic nature and the natural world around us.

Without a sea change, we're on a course to bomb or global-warm ourselves back to a more primal state. And if we do, is there any guarantee we would remake our societies on the partnership model instead of the dominator model—especially under such harsh and traumatizing circumstances? Maybe this is our life cycle. Humans will keep being who they are, acting out their fate, like all flora and fauna. Population growth magnified by science and technology, followed by population collapse brought about by a tearing away from our roots in the Earth and the Tao. Are we doomed to endlessly ride the same Ferris wheel? Change will happen. Do we have the compassion, wisdom, resourcefulness, and resilience to make it a life- and love-enhancing one?

David Korten, in his book *Change the Story, Change the Future*, says we took a wrong path 5,000 years ago. He's optimistic that we're ready to choose the right one.

> *Earth birthed our species some two hundred thousand years ago. We acknowledged our dependence on her and honored her as our sacred Earth Mother. Our sense of separation began around 3000 BCE with the rise of imperial civilizations. It accelerated over the most recent four hundred years as modern science began to advance our godlike powers to manipulate, suppress, and exploit*

her. In our forgetfulness of what we are and whence we came, we behave as our Earth Mother's prodigal children acting in adolescent rebellion.

As is common for adolescents, our ability to reshape our world developed faster than our capacity to act with wisdom and emotional maturity. With a naïve sense of invincibility, we recklessly tested the limits of newfound abilities, unmindful that special abilities come with special responsibilities.

Hope lies in the evidence that we are reawakening to what I believe to be a fundamental truth of our existence. We humans, like all other beings, are both product and instrument of creation, not its purpose. We belong to Earth, and our health and well-being are inseparable from her health and well-being.[53]

Korten offers concrete ideas for how we can abandon the "Sacred Money and Markets story" before it's too late and start inhabiting the "Sacred Life and Living Earth story." By vesting power in people, households, and communities and promoting "local self-reliance," he believes we can find our way back to the Grand Harmony.

I want to believe Korten, but the 2016 presidential election rattled the fragile optimism I'd been carefully tending. I spent that night pacing and crying.

If Hilary Clinton had been elected, I would have drunk the wine I took to the home of friends and celebrated the fact of our first woman president just as I celebrated the fact of our first black president. But Hilary seemed to have lost her way somewhere during her extensive career in public life. She and Obama and a long line of presidents before them were leading us (and following us) in a slow but sure slide into oligarchy in which nothing mattered but materialism, greed, and power. Wall Street, along with the big banks and corporations have been inexorably displacing our democracy. At least Trump's election clarified conditions, woke people up to the emergency, and galvanized them.

There were plenty of reasons for my horror at Trump's election, but the most nightmarish, the one that I viscerally didn't want to look at and that filled me with fear, nausea, and hopelessness was what I sensed as the hollowing out of the heart of America. This goes deeper than politics or issues.

Speaking at an awards show, Meryl Streep asked the same question that had been haunting me: When all America saw Donald Trump mimic and mock a handicapped reporter, why did his candidacy ever go past that?

The spate of zombie movies was so apt. Heartless, mindless, ravenous beings. People live in a stupor induced by their addiction to TV, Internet, video games, talk radio, and the celebrity culture. Constant noise and distraction leave no time or space to *think*. They cheerfully watch reality TV shows like *The Apprentice* in which people are bullied and humiliated and then fired. They gravitate to sensationalized, often fake news programs where they absorb callous, coarse, racist, misogynistic rants. They *play* at brutality and cruelty with video games. Hard-core pornography at their fingertips fuels the hatred and disrespect of women. People want to be famous and they don't care what for. They want to be rich and they don't care how they make their money.

Nicholas Carr published a book in 2011 called *The Shallows*. It's about the effect on our brains and our lives by constant exposure to the Internet. The title lets you know where he's going with it. Carr had to completely unplug from the Internet for a year in order to be capable of writing the book. At the time he decided to begin the project, he confesses, he was unable to sit down and *read* an entire book because of the Internet's influence on him. He was down to being able to absorb only scattered sound bites.

You would think that access to the Internet would provide vast new resources to scholars and writers. But Carr learned the contrary. Internet search engines sort information by popularity—the sites that get the most hits rise to the first page. Everyone doing research began citing the same sources, over and over again. Wandering through the stacks of libraries, picking up books you weren't looking for is more likely to open up new ideas and expand thinking than confining oneself to the Internet.

I can't blame people for seeking out distractions in this chaotic world. The Internet, the media, technology, and opioids are the opiate of the people.

Global warming is inescapable. Looking out at forest, ocean, and sky, my T'ai Chi practices are tainted by sadness and remorse. Where will we go for refuge when nature can no longer provide it? Climate change threatens the very idea of posterity. Even if we manage to find a way to control it and keep the temperature rise within livable limits, much unnecessary suffering is already happening and will escalate in the meantime.

We're surrounded by constant war. We watch it on screens, hear about it on the radio, and read about it in print. Everyone who goes to war is damaged by it, if not killed. Combatants come back and their wounds—physical and psychological—have a ripple effect on their families, friends, coworkers, and communities. Many more combatants and collaterally injured civilians in the countries where we wage these wars are having the same effect.

War uproots whole populations. At this writing, sixty-eight million people are displaced. They become refugees and immigrants. Mass immigration strains the economic capacity and the tolerance capacity of the sanctuary countries. Xenophobia is stoked. The refugees of global warming exacerbate the problem and will increasingly do so. In the early 1980s I attended a lecture on the people of Appalachia. The researcher had discovered that even though the inhabitants of the villages shared the same racial, ethnic, and socioeconomic background, those living in one valley saw their counterparts in the next valley as "other" and held virulent suspicion and hostility toward them. This tells us something about human nature. How much more "other" is someone of a different race, religion, and culture?

All these challenges will bring out the best in some and the worst in others. Have we created a world of such dizzying unpredictability, insecurity, and violence that it exceeds most humans' capacity to adapt? It doesn't surprise me that one reflexive response is to pull in, hunker down with your tribe, and man the barricades.

Throughout the presidential campaign I saw two primary factors in play—misogyny and racism. People weren't ready to elevate a woman to our highest office, especially after eight years of a black man's occupying that place. Resistance to the rising power of women and backlash against Obama made a formidable combination. Women and people of color are in the ascendant and white males are losing their primacy (a hopeful trend), but they won't give it up without a fight. The patriarchy is under attack and knows it. They are doubling down.

The selfish, conscienceless extremes of the Tea Party—enabled by gerrymandering and the suppression of voting rights—has left a vacuum of ethical, moral leadership in the Republican Party. That vacuum was filled by a power-hungry opportunist who is another ethical and moral vacuum. A vacuum filling a vacuum? One of the laws that Trump defies is a law of physics.

I understand that Trump's win was assisted by the gutting of the American middle class by mechanization and international trade deals. But many Tea Partiers are not poor or struggling; they're greedy. They want to protect and increase their wealth and privilege and don't want to pay taxes to support the society that supports them. They have no concern for how the people around them are doing. And don't care if they live in a democracy, an oligarchy, or a dictatorship as long as they thrive. Toto pulled back the curtain again and again during a year-long campaign; the con man was exposed. So I can only conclude Trump hooked many of his supporters on one or more of these things: misogyny, racism, greed, xenophobia, or narcissism—all symptoms of our dominator culture.

Of all the people insulted by Trump's election, women are at the top of the list—half the human race. The Women's March was born in and fueled by outrage yet it upheld love and peace. It was the perfect example of yin leading, supported by yang. The world recognized and joined in, and continues to in succeeding Marches. The instinct for self-preservation has catalyzed millions of humans across the planet to demand the return to a balanced, sustainable partnership culture. It's natural that women will be taking the lead now, joined by men who comprehend the flip that has to take place. In its most extreme state, yang gives rise to yin.

The #MeToo movement—the outing of so many men in government, industry, academia, and private life for sexually harassing and abusing women—is a welcome sign of genuine revolution. I'm continually astounded by the sudden about-face of society—not only believing survivors of sexual assault, but exacting serious consequences for perpetrators. The confirmation of Brett Kavanaugh to the Supreme Court was a last-ditch pulling out of all the stops by an angry, besieged patriarchy, and will further awaken the sleeping dragon. The zeitgeist is indeed reversing, and I believe the trend will gain momentum over the next generations.

The LGBTQ movement is also part of the feminine tsunami. One of LGBTQ's precious gifts is that it frees everyone to be whatever combination of masculine and feminine they want, at any given time. Who's to say who's a man and who's a woman?

The LGBTQ movement is the feminine principle at work in the form of noninterference—Wu Wei—allowing people to be who they are instead of mindlessly, cruelly flattening them into the cookie-cutter shapes of patriarchal convention, extreme male or extreme female. The Goddess is never just the Goddess; the God is never just the God. We can't afford to be separating, segregating, and dividing ourselves anymore. We just don't have time for it. We need all hands on deck for this historic transformational effort.

I have hope for the global upwelling of the feminine spirit. The movement enfolds all the other movements for human rights, human dignity, peace, and love—for oneself, fellow humans, and the planet.

I joined the Resistance the day after the election. It became another given—a calling—in my life. I had plans, but had to make room for another one. When I'm weary and depressed by the daily pummeling, I think of myself as a bee in a bee hive or an ant in an ant hill. I drop out, move to the side to rest and repair, knowing millions of others will still be buzzing and marching. When I'm ready (often renewed by time in nature), I rejoin the work. We're in a battle for the soul of America.

I'm not a parent and am not in close touch with young people. But my friends who are parents and grandparents tell me the youth are growing up whole and healthy, aware and motivated. (My sample is limited. I hear and read about the other side too.) It's a wonder that any children can not only survive but even thrive— with hearts intact—under current conditions. My generation and the two coming up will have to reverse the soul-devouring trends if balance is to be restored. The problem is so intractable because it's on the inside, not the outside. Humans will have to transcend themselves. Or maybe not. We were in a partnership culture before; so that means we already have it in us and it can roll around again. We contain the seeds of our own destruction, yes, and we also contain the seeds of our regeneration.

Because our illness is internal, healing will have to happen from the inside out, starting with each one of us and radiating to the larger world.

> *Cultivated in the individual, character will become genuine;*
> *Cultivated in the family, character will become abundant;*
> *Cultivated in the village, character will multiply;*
> *Cultivated in the state, character will prosper;*
> *Cultivated in the world, character will become universal.*[54]

All of us come with impulses for both good and evil, and over the course of a lifetime we act on both. But what determines the general direction of an individual's character? Does it arc toward extinguishing life and love or does it arc toward feeding life and love? Nature and nurture have their say. And I think we have to pin our hopes on one other factor—our willingness to look honestly at ourselves, to get wise to ourselves and use an elastic, transcendent awareness to work with our *whole* selves to bend that arc toward healing and away from harming. I'm not sure it's possible for us to be unconsciously good like the people of Laotse's Grand Harmony. Starting from where we are, we'll have to combine conscious and unconscious to enter a state of balance again. And I've learned that the two together are stronger than either by itself.

I am a circle. I have a birth, a life, and a death; as does my species, the planet, the solar system, and the cosmos. Circles revolve within circles; wheels turn within wheels, the largest exerting its pull on the smallest, and the smallest on the largest. There's no stopping it. I don't know how long I or my species will live. In the meantime, all I can do is strive for personal balance, add my small weight to help level the human wheel, and inhale as much joy and fulfillment from life as I can. "To finish the moment, to find the journey's end in every step of the road, to live the greatest number of good hours, is wisdom. ...The only ballast I know is a respect to the present hour."[55]

Deep inside me, where it would hide unnoticed if I let it, is a bottomless grief for the unavoidable decay, loss, and death that's embedded in life; and for the avoidable folly and pain of human existence. I accept it. I bring its presence into mine with tears. Yet just as deep is the primal loyalty I feel toward my species and planet. I know that humans are simultaneously flawed and divine. So I can't stop myself from hoping that humans will, within one of our wheels within wheels, have a renewal of life- and love-affirming culture. If there are enough of us, billions wanting to live full lives, blossoming in a caring society. Success or failure in this endeavor is ultimately the same. Courage is our victory.

CHAPTER ELEVEN NOTES

1. Jonathan Star, transl. and ed., *Tao Te Ching: The Definitive Edition*, (New York: Jeremy P. Tarcher/Penguin, 2001), Ch. 52, p. 65.

2. Gia-fu Feng and Jane English, transl., *Tao Te Ching*, (New York: Random House Vintage Books, 1972), Ch. 52.

3. Stephen Mitchell, ed., *Tao Te Ching: A New English Version*, (New York: Harper Perennial Modern Classics, 2006) Ch. 53.

4. Chang Chung-yuan, transl. and ed., *Tao: A New Way of Thinking*, (New York: Harper & Row Harper Colophon Books, 1975), Ch. 37, p. 104.

5. Ibid.

6. Chang, Ch. 10, p. 33.

7. Chuangtse, quoted in Lin Yutang, transl. and ed., *The Wisdom of Laotse*, (New York: Random House Modern Library, 1948), Ch. 50. p. 241.

8. Lin Yutang, transl. and ed., *The Wisdom of Laotse*, (New York: Random House Modern Library, 1948), Ch. 50, p. 233.

9. Ralph Waldo Emerson, sermon quoted in editor's introductory note to "Self-Reliance," in *The Annotated Emerson*, David Mikics, ed., (Cambridge, MA: The Belknap Press of Harvard University Press, 2012), p. 160.

10. Emerson, "Self-Reliance," in *The Annotated Emerson*, p. 165.

11. Emerson, "Experience," in *The Annotated Emerson*, p. 237.

12. Emerson, Journal 1845 and 1850-51, quoted in note #81 in "Experience," in *The Annotated Emerson*, p. 244.

13. Emerson, "Power," in *The Annotated Emerson*, p. 440.

14. Emerson, letter to Mary Moody, quoted in *Emerson: The Mind on Fire*, Robert D. Richardson, Jr. (Berkeley: University of California Press, 1995), p. 88.

15. Ralph Waldo Emerson, "Compensation," in *Essays, Poems, Addresses* (New York: Walter J. Black Classics Club, 1941), p. 151.

16. Lin Yutang, Ch. 77, p. 305-6.

17. Emerson, "Compensation," in *Essays, Poems, Addresses*, p. 155-6.

18. Ibid., p. 156.

19. Ibid., p. 157.
20. Ibid., p. 152.
21. Ibid., p. 152-3.
22. Ibid., p. 153.
23. Ibid., p. 154.
24. Ibid., p. 154-5.
25. Ibid., p. 165.
26. Ibid., p. 159.
27. Ibid., p. 167.
28. Ibid., p. 168.
29. Emerson, "Fate," in *The Annotated Emerson*, p. 427.
30. Emerson, "Compensation," in *Essays, Poems, Addresses*, p. 166.
31. Ibid., p. 162-3.
32. Emerson, "The Over-Soul," in *Essays, Poems, Addresses*, p. 221.
33. Emerson, "Nature," in *The Annotated Emerson*, p. 70.
34. Lin Yutang, Ch. 9, p. 79 and Ch. 67, p. 291.
35. Feng and English, Ch. 24.
36. Feng and English, Ch. 22 and 24.
37. Mitchell, Ch. 26.
38. Min Jiayin, ed., *The Chalice and the Blade in Chinese Culture: Gender Relations and Social Models*, (Beijing: China Social Sciences Publishing House, 1995) p. 230-1.
39. Min Jiayin, p. 590-91.
40. Min Jiayin, p. 592.
41. Lin Yutang, Ch. 65, p. 285.
42. Lin Yutang, Ch. 8, p. 76.
43. Lin Yutang, Ch. 78, p. 306.
44. Lin Yutang, Ch. 32, p. 172.
45. Lin Yutang, Ch. 6, p. 64.
46. Lin Yutang, Ch. 66, p. 290.
47. Laotse, *Tao Te Ching*, Ch. 61, various translations.
48. Laotse, *Tao Te Ching*, Ch. 69, various translations.
49. Laotse, *Tao Te Ching*, Ch. 79, various translations.
50. Lin Yutang, Ch. 45, p. 223.
51. Lin Yutang, Ch. 76, p. 305.
52. Lin Yutang, Ch. 36, p. 191.

53. David C. Korten, *Change the Story, Change the Future: A Living Economy for a Living Earth*, (Oakland, CA: Berrett-Koehler, 2015), p. 75-6.
54. Lin Yutang, Ch. 54, p. 249.
55. Emerson, "Experience," in *The Annotated Emerson*, p. 234.

Margaret Emerson

ACKNOWLEDGMENTS

I'm grateful for friends who listened to me, offered their thoughts, and spurred my thinking and writing over the years of work on this book—the people in my T'ai Chi classes, the members of my women's group and of Thursday Night Reflections at the Humboldt Unitarian Universalist Fellowship. I thank Bonnie MacGregor for inviting me to present versions of chapters from *Laotse, Waldo, and Me* at Sunday services at the Fellowship. With perfect timing, Terry Albini and June Sawyers sent me a birthday gift of David Mikics's *The Annotated Emerson*. Also with serendipitous timing, Tom Torma gave me *The Chalice and the Blade in Chinese Culture*. Caroline Isaacs and Jane Levy read the manuscript and offered helpful, encouraging comments. David Marshak responded chapter by chapter with a writer's eye and gave me gentle, astute suggestions that helped me bring the book to its completion.

The Morris Graves Foundation awarded me a 3-week writing residency in pristine nature. I owe special thanks to its dedicated stewards, Robert and Desiree Yarber. I honed much of the final chapter while overlooking a lily-bejeweled lake surrounded by old-growth forest.

Made in the USA
Middletown, DE
24 August 2019